contents

Foreword **vii**
Preface **ix**
Introduction **1**
Disclaimer time ... **5**

Part I: Getting into the world of gin
Chapter 1   The extraordinary (and colourful) history of gin **9**
Chapter 2   What is gin? **25**
Chapter 3   The art of tasting gin **47**
Chapter 4   Gin lingo **69**

Part II: Delving into all the parts that make the whole
Chapter 5   How gin is made **81**
Chapter 6   It's all about the juniper ... **105**
Chapter 7   The best of the botanicals **119**
Chapter 8   Choosing your ideal mixer **143**
Chapter 9   The finishing touches – your garnish guide **153**

Part III: Building your bar skills
Chapter 10   Mastering mixology **169**
Chapter 11   Home bar essentials (and a few non-essentials...) **179**

Part IV: Mixing drinks
Chapter 12   The classic G&T **201**
Chapter 13   The gin martini **217**
Chapter 14   Cocktail of the moment: the negroni **241**
Chapter 15   The resurgence of the cocktail (and its inebriated history) **247**

One last shot ... **279**
Gin musings ... **281**
Acknowledgements **285**
About the author **287**

foreword

When I was first approached by Clare to write a foreword for this book, I reflected on what my personal journey has been with not only gin, but also spirits in general. What credentials do I possibly have that make me suitable to perform such a duty?

In 2001, I had my very first introduction to the magic of distilleries, the wonders that different ingredients can do when brought together and the history lessons of brand stories when I started on my first day with Diageo.

Diageo is a global drinks company that has enabled many people like me to become spirits lovers by developing a passion for the what and how of mixing drinks, creating cocktails, and learning how to drink 'neat'.

As a young man from the suburbs, my introduction to alcohol was beer in football club change rooms. The concept of drinking spirits was only for when you couldn't stomach any more beer!

Fast-forward 30-something years from those formative days and my indulgence with alcohol is now all about taste, experience and brand affiliation.

While working for Diageo, I was first introduced to a gin called Tanqueray. The privilege of the staff account allowed me to step up and experience a natural progression to 'Tanq 10' with its tall and beautiful green bottle. Both mixed with tonic or, alternatively, as a refreshing mix with lime and soda, I fell in love with the concept of gin. But, even then, gin was still a mystery and I was a bit confused as to whether its identity was as an old person's drink or a hip new alternative to vodka.

In 2013, I moved spirit companies and began working for the Bacardi family at Bacardi-Martini Australia. I needed to move my alliance from the green bottle of Tanqueray to the stunning blue bottle of Bombay Sapphire.

Immediately, the name conjured up ideas of wealth and prestige and, upon my first taste, I was hooked. I had found my new drink of choice!

This time coincided with an emerging new category in the market – Australian craft spirits – and the category leading this new charge was gin.

I became a secret admirer of brands such as Four Pillars, Archie Rose, West Winds and Melbourne Gin Company.

It was these local distilleries that immersed themselves in pushing the boundaries with the botanicals they blended, and that quickly caught the consumers' attention. The names of the brands, their stories, the characters behind the brands and, finally, the brand homes that became legitimate places for us to sample, learn and become brand ambassadors all helped cement their popularity.

I left Bacardi three years ago to become the GM of ALM (Australian Liquor Marketers), and my passion for gin hasn't lapsed – nor has it for the dozens of retailers proudly showcasing over 60 different gin brands on their shelves. Gin is the fastest growing spirits category right now and when I was first pointed in the direction of Heathcote Gin from a retailer who has stores in that region, I just had to learn more.

And so it was that I met Clare Voitin – a working mum following her passion with an abundance of energy, raw in her knowledge of the landscape of the liquor industry but with a huge appetite to learn. And it was then that I tried my first Heathcote Gin – Navy Strength to be exact, with a slice of lime and Fever-Tree tonic.

I was hooked by the beautiful but simple bottle and label, with ingredients sourced from a region rich in its wine history. The more of the range I tried, the more I believed in its future. I had never had a drinking experience like the one when I had the Heathcote Shiraz Gin mixed with Capi Cola – the flavours, the colour and, yet again, another magnificent drinking experience.

Clare and Heathcote Gin are on their way now and this book is as much testament to her hard work as it is to the passion she has for the category and the education she wants to impart on both the experienced and the novice gin drinker.

Enjoy the book, but please do so with whatever gin you have fallen in love with, in a glass loaded with ice and your favourite mixer and fruit accompaniment.

I proudly look forward to recommending this book to anyone looking to learn the art of gin ... and everything that comes with it!

Jeremy Goodale
GM, Australian Liquor Marketers

preface

If you had asked me 20 years ago what I knew about gin, my mind would have pretty much drawn a blank. I enjoyed a drop (or few) on ice with a half-decent tonic, but other than that my experience and knowledge of gin was rather limited, and certainly not worthy of an intelligent dinner conversation ... or a book.

Had you suggested that I would end up being the founder of a gin brand, based on an idea formed over a long lunch and one-too-many exceptional Heathcote reds, I would have probably choked on (and wasted) whatever I was drinking at the time. But life deals interesting cards – in my case, that can lead into an unforgettable afternoon, during which the seed of an idea can be so simply sewn into my creative (and, some might say, crazy) mind. That seed grew into Heathcote Gin, and starting up my own gin brand from scratch has been, to say the least, a fascinating journey, with a few steep learning curves along the way.

Fortunately, I have a deep love of learning. Combined with a passion for sustainable farming, working on the land alongside Mother Nature and being a strong (sometimes stubborn) advocate for consuming all things local, the birth of Heathcote Gin could, at a stretch, be seen as a logical next step in my agricultural, foodie and farming journey.

The beauty of gin is in its diversity. Unlike other spirits, where you're somewhat limited in how much you can play around with the flavours, aromas and ingredients, gin offers the producer creative scope to come up with exciting new variations on one of the world's oldest spirits. Indeed, making gin represents an opportunity to develop a signature style and flavour. In the case of Heathcote Gin, it provides an intricate, yet sophisticated platform to showcase the beauty of a local region, and discover ways to create a new hero, found directly in nature, patiently waiting for its true potential to be revealed.

What I love most about creating a local, regional gin is the journey of exploring our local botanicals, the discovery of what may lie on our region's doorstep and how this discovery may become an exciting opportunity to share something special beyond the local community. Simply put, making gin using the landscape of our region as the palate is not only exciting but also unique. Nowhere in the world can a spirit be created quite like the one we've been inspired to create from Heathcote.

Gin doesn't need years of storage, fermentation and maturation to deliver its own version of excellence. I'm known at times for my lack of patience, so delivering a product that doesn't require me to wait around for years to reach its full maturity suits me well.

Gin, in my humble opinion, is a hidden treasure that, enjoyed sensibly, can mark significant moments, help celebrate an important occasion or even just be enjoyed for what it is – gin.

For me, gin marks the moment when the day is almost done. The gentle clink of my favourite gin glass, the tumbling of ice, the delicious sound of fresh tonic bubbles pouring with the hero of the moment – gin – all of which bring the occasion together to create a small moment of magic.

Gin's colourful history is a story in itself. First conceived in the early 1300s, gin has had a rocky ride from then to now. Considered an extremely unhealthy addiction for many during most of its history, it was most likely responsible for foolish accidents, broken relationships, penniless existences and even untimely deaths. But, like all good things, if enjoyed in moderation, you have a fascinating drop that, in most cases, has a story to tell.

In the case of Heathcote Gin, I want to share something of what I've learnt on my own gin journey. Where does one begin with gin production, and what are the steps, hurdles and processes along the way? Too often, we can get caught up on all the detail and miss the beauty of the story – and the story is everything, to the point where such a tale can draw out the essence of the gin itself. Why are the botanicals and sometimes even the region the gin comes from so important? What has inspired so many others around the world to take the same bold leap I did and produce their own version of gin excellence? And how do you pick the gin – and method of drinking it – that's right for you?

This book will lay it all out, from the beginning of gin's creation to the here and now. I will share with you some simple tips on how to recognise a

good gin, as well as providing a source of inspiration and motivation to try different gins, and learn to appreciate the subtle differences from one gin to the next. And, of course, I tell you how to mix a few drinks featuring gin – from the perfect G&T to the martini that's perfect for you.

Like a fine wine, gin also exudes its own personality. When produced with a region in mind, you are enjoying the fruits and botanicals of that region. In the case of Heathcote Gin, the story begins in the region of Heathcote, a beautiful – yet still largely undiscovered – part of the world, tucked away in the heart of rural Victoria, Australia.

To be perfectly honest with you, I am by no means a gin expert. Instead, I like to think of myself as an explorer and a guide. My role here is to help you appreciate gin for what it is – an exquisite, fascinating spirit that has a lot more to it than you may think.

So I invite you to join me on this gin journey. I hope the pages that follow enlighten and entertain you, ignite your deeper interest in the world's best spirit and inspire you to find your own creative journey. At the very least, hopefully you'll learn a thing or two about gin.

So here's cheers to you and your gin journey!

Clare Voitin
clare@theheathcotegin.com.au
Facebook @HeathcoteGin
Instagram @Heathcote.Gin

introduction

Unfortunately (or maybe fortunately), I can't quite remember my first gin and tonic (G&T). To be honest, it was probably an experience I've chosen to forget, simply because I was young, foolish and unable to afford something a little bit more sophisticated than what my paltry budget reduced me to drinking.

The classic G&T is one of the world's most popular mixed drinks. Simple in its preparation and designed to encourage swift consumption, a G&T has always been considered the perfect summer drink. No more, I cry…

Gin has taken the world stage as one of the fastest growing spirits in the world – and no longer are we just delegating gin drinking to the warmer months. Why? Who really knows? But I don't hear anyone complaining.

Maybe it's due to the courageous efforts of a few of the world's largest brands to ride the peaks and troughs of interest (or lack thereof) in gin. Possibly it's the newfound 'love of local' that has inspired local gins brands and distillers to come out of their garages and no longer hide their backyard stills to showcase their own version of juniper excellence. One might even argue that the health conscious are turning to gin due to the presence of botanicals that carry antioxidants and, in some cases, super-food status.

Whatever the reasons, gin is now on-trend and a much-loved spirit – and people simply cannot get enough of it. Liquor retailers are now burdened with finding extra space to add more new gins to their shelves to keep up with demand, and gin lovers are buying up big for their gin bars at home.

In the 1990s and early 2000s, only a handful of big names played in the gin space. Fast-forward 20 years and those iconic bottles are now spending their days on the bottom shelves to make way for the generous range of locally made craft varieties that are exciting, funky and new.

Of course, we must salute those pioneers of gin that have stood tall and strong through the 'thick and thin' of gin fads and, to this day, represent not only a wonderful history of gin but also a standard that new and emerging producers can be inspired by to deliver their own version of excellence.

Through these old and new players, gin has fast-tracked its way to centre stage and has no intention of moving to the side anytime soon. Gin is bold and brassy, sexy and delicious, and – despite what some party-pooping critics may say – the market is by no means saturated. Compared to the global (and local) wine industry, gin is still well and truly micro-niched, with a long and exciting, onward and upward journey ahead.

Gin is not just booze in a bottle. Gin is an exquisite work of art. Gin is a creative endeavour that begins with a simple idea. It has a place of origin and carries a story – which the creator is usually only too happy to share with any passionate gin lover who dares to ask where it all began. That story usually begins with the botanicals, and each botanical in gin has an origin and history. The choice of which are selected begins with the gin maker, with each selection then carefully fine-tuned through much trial and error. Sometimes, it can take years for the gin artiste to produce their version of the 'perfect gin' and, more often than not, its birthplace and story is what creates its unique point of difference. If you dig a little deeper into the history of your favourite gin, you may well find a fascinating story behind how each botanical came to be such an integral ingredient.

Gin is built on a dream. With love and passion, and the determination to strive for perfection, this dream is underpinned by the need for acceptance from others who share similar affections for such creations – to make that spirit in a bottle have a purpose and 'raison d'être'.

The myths and misconceptions around gin are many. Whether those stories are created from boredom (not enough gin) or inebriation (too much gin), we'll never know.

Regardless of what you may or may not know, this book is designed to guide, educate and – above all – entertain you, with a view to leaving you at the end pages inspired to try new gins and not sit on your predictable, more traditional favourites. If creating your best version of a spirit in a bottle is on your bucket list, I hope this book encourages you to fulfil that dream of having your own gin someday.

At the time of writing this book, I was working harder than ever on Heathcote Gin, a business and brand that began over that long lunch with an old friend. The seed that was planted during that lunch has well and truly grown, to become a much-loved Australian premium craft gin enjoyed and appreciated by so many in such a short time.

And that, my friends, is the wonder and beauty of gin.

disclaimer time ...

If I've discovered one thing about gin, it's that drunken folklore doesn't always allow the truth to get in the way of a damn good story. And who can blame these storytelling legends, who have probably thrown down a drink or few in their endeavour to attach themselves to a new imbibe in a cheeky effort to grab five minutes of fame?

If only they knew the impact of their drunken tales, and the value of having one sober fella at the table properly documenting these stories.

Isn't hindsight a wonderful thing?

Hours upon hours have been spent researching for this book, digging deep to find the stories worth sharing, ensuring that what you read in this book is as accurate as it can possibly be. And throughout the researching for and writing of this book, I've learned that booze and storytelling can make for compelling reading – even more so for the stories from back in the day, when regulating alcohol was such a near-impossible task for the authorities.

What is written here is as good as gin gospel can get – and the writer was sober the entire way through! Where any part of history appears a little too influenced by distorted truths and legendary tales, I've done my best to make that clear for you, the reader.

One final disclaimer – when it comes to distilling gin, please don't try this at home. Not only is it illegal, but it can also be dangerous. And that's just the botanicals, I'm referring to ...

Putting aside all of this, keep in mind that this is a book written for you. Whether you're an avid gin lover, already armed with an in-depth knowledge and appreciation of this wonderful spirit, or you're a new gin drinker with a thirst for gin knowledge and inspiration, this book is just for you.

Every great gin has a story worth sharing. Every cocktail or G&T can usually attach itself to a memorable occasion with family or friends. Every passion has a purpose. May this book further enhance your passion for gin and take you on an awesome new gin journey.

PART I
GETTING INTO THE WORLD OF GIN

CHAPTER 1

the extraordinary (and colourful) history of gin

'The Gin Palace' (George Cruikshank)

I drank so much gin last night I woke up with a London Dry accent.

You might be mistaken for thinking the brilliant genius responsible for the creation of gin originated from England – after all, gin is considered England's national spirit. However, gin – or at least its earlier incarnation – was first made in Holland. It then found its way to England – and (not a moment too soon) the rest of the world.

genever becomes gin

The distant beginnings of gin occurred sometime around the 13th century, with reference made to a spirit flavoured with 'genever' in a Flemish manuscript. The spirit that became known as genever (also spelt jenever) began to be more widely produced in Holland over 400 years ago, and is considered the ancestor of gin. 'Jeneverbes' is the Dutch name for 'juniper' and it is through its use of the juniper berry that genever derived its name. By the 1600s, the Dutch were producing genever in earnest, with dozens of distilleries popping up in and around Amsterdam alone.

Genever spirit was made from three ingredients – malt wine, alcohol and water. The method behind the concoction of the malt wine was handed down through generations, from father to son, and it is this tradition that formed the heart and soul of the genever spirit. The second ingredient – alcohol – was flavoured with a good amount of juniper berries, designed to camouflage the highly unpleasant taste of the malt wine as much as accommodate the lack of refined distilling techniques available at the time[1].

The use of juniper berries is what creates the connection between 'genever' and 'gin'. By the 1700s, as producers started to drop the malt wine and refine their production techniques, the spirit took on a new form and function – now (affectionately) known as gin.

As with most spirits produced way back when, the consumption of genever was justified based on its 'medicinal value'. Folklore tells the story that, as word spread about this new medicinal elixir and cure-all, the number of 'patients' with hypochondria rose sharply, all keen to try this new medicine that not only cured ailments (real or perceived), but also tasted delicious. While this may or may not be quite true, I do consider the story worthy of a special mention here.

the english get on board

The English discovered gin during the Anglo–Dutch Wars (1652–1674) and perhaps as early as the Thirty Years' War (1618–1648), after seeing Dutch soldiers drinking genever gin to boost their morale before battle. In fact, the all-too-familiar term 'Dutch courage' was borne around this time.

Soon after, gin made its way across to England, where it rapidly gained popularity and became a necessity of sorts, not only for the enjoyment derived when one consumed such a pleasant-tasting spirit, but also for its perceived medicinal value.

Gin was also deemed a healthier alternative to plain water, particularly in the cities where the quality of the drinking water was unclean, unfiltered

---

1   Today genever is still produced and best described as the perfect blend of whiskey and gin. In 2008, the Dutch Government and the EU officially created an AOC *(apellation d'origine controlee)*, which permits the production of genever in Holland, Belgium and specific parts of France and Germany.

and dirty. As a distilled alcohol with medicinal benefits, gin was the drink of choice, and a tidy excuse to keep on drinking.

As with most good things, gin became so popular that, by around 1720, experts estimate up to a quarter of the households in London were producing their own gin. What became known as the 'Gin Craze' brought its own share of social problems. Many at the time argued London society was spiralling out of control, with people self-medicating for their perceived ailments, drinkers becoming addicted to the spirit and most enjoying this new cheap 'distilled' thrill for the sheer pleasure of it.

Gin was deemed responsible for the dramatic spike in crime, prostitution, misery and depression – and even higher death rates and lower birth rates. Mothers were accused of forgetting their responsibilities, due to their extended periods of inebriation, and not caring for their young children and newborn babies.

In 1723, the rate of deaths outnumbered birth rates in London and remained higher for the next decade. A disturbing percentage of babies died before the age of five and fertility rates were also lower – all argued to be due to the excessive consumption of gin.

Historians note that gin was used to hush the babes, calm the mothers and keep the menfolk distracted from the realities of their time. As is often the case, even today, women were the ones who seemed to suffer the worst of the judgement with gin, earning the nicknames of the 'Ladies Delight', 'Mother Gin', 'Madam Geneva' or 'Mother's Ruin', some of which still hold a familiar ring today.

keeping the english under control

Based on these (perceived and actual) ill-effects of gin, the government stepped in and took action.

A series of Gin Acts were passed. In 1729, the first of five major Gin Acts was introduced. This Act increased duty on gin sales, but a loophole was soon found by those desperate to continue their addictive habits. The Act enforced higher duties on spirits that had 'juniper berries, or other fruit, spices or ingredients' added to the spirit.

William Hogarth – Gin Lane (1751)

By avoiding the addition of these ingredients, home brewers continued to produce their preferred spirit known as 'Parliamentary brandy'. This meant legitimate distillers were penalised for their honesty, while illicit producers were running thriving businesses.

The Gin Act of 1736 taxed retail gin sales at 20 shillings a gallon and legislated that any distiller must do so only under a licence, with an annual fee of 50 pounds. Without such a licence, making your own gin was illegal. (At the time, 50 pounds was equivalent to an annual wage for a skilled worker.) Legislators hoped these changes would make the cost of producing gin – and so the price of gin – prohibitive. Instead, the distilling industry went further underground, thus creating a bigger problem. As a result, the quality of gin (or variations of gin-like substances) sunk to a new base level. No longer was gin made the 'right' way, and other cheaper ingredients and flavours were used, such as sawdust, turpentine or (worse still) sulphuric acid instead of juniper.

The Gin Act was revised in 1737, and encouraged informants to be rewarded for dobbing in an illicit producer. This caused near riots, and assaults and attacks on informants. In the meantime, gin sales continued to rise.

A further amendment of the Gin Act (in 1738) attempted to outlaw gin production completely, and made it illegal to attack the informers dobbing in those who produced the gin that now wasn't allowed to be produced. Despite this, gin production continued (heading further underground). Drinking dens were abundant and inebriation, crime and early deaths were no longer the exception to the rule.

Creative minds were also at play here, when Captain Dudley Bradstreet came up with (I have to admit) a brilliant idea. After researching the latest interpretation of the Gin Act, he found a loophole that required an informer to know the name of the person renting the property from where the gin was illegally sold. This was the only way the authorities could break in and arrest the illegal gin seller.

Captain Bradstreet, therefore, had an anonymous friend rent a house in London. He nailed a picture of a cat in the window and made it known that gin would be available from a cat in the alley the following day.

The Captain moved in with enough food to eat and an abundance of gin to sell, and then barricaded himself into the house.

The next day, people lined up in front of the 'Puss and Mew' window with the picture of the cat. The customers would whisper 'Puss', and wait for the affirmative response of 'Mew' from the Captain. On this signal, the patron would push money through a slot in the cat's mouth and, in return, the Captain would pour gin down a small pipe that was hidden under the cat's paw. Customers would either bring a cup or just hold their mouth under the pipe to receive their gin. You have to admit – it's genius. And while the authorities knew what was going on, they were powerless to act, because they didn't know the name of the person renting the house.

Captain Bradstreet profiteered for a number of months before copycat salesmen took on the idea, forcing him to move on.

All the while, the drinking and selling of gin was getting so messy that informers were getting harassed and, in some cases, murdered for their tell-tattling ways. Even magistrates gave up trying to punish the wrongdoers for fear of their own safety, as well as the fact that it was near impossible keeping up to effectively impose the law.

And so the Gin Craze continued to spiral out of control.

By 1742, over 8 million gallons of gin were being produced a year. That translates to over 8 litres on average per person being consumed. Of these 8 million gallons, only 40 gallons of licensed (legitimate) gin was sold.

By now, London was in crisis. Birth rates had plummeted even further while death rates continued to rise, including 1 in 5 infant deaths per annum. Alcoholism was clearly a problem, but gin was not entirely responsible. The Gin Craze was born out of poverty. Gin (and, let's not forget, particularly bad gin – the turpentine-based stuff), was the spirit of choice to help someone forget their suffering and despair. It was cheap, readily available and numbed the pain and harsh reality of the poverty-stricken life in the slums that so many endured.

In 1751, a new and improved Gin Act was passed. This Act somewhat cleaned up the industry and created a semblance of balance and control, by lowering the licence fee but forcing distillers to sell only to registered and respected licensed retailers.

By 1757, a change in the local economy helped bring further order to the chaos around gin. Poor harvests meant grain prices went up, which also forced the price of food up and wages down. No longer could the poor afford to eat and drink gin. Because the base alcohol for gin traditionally comes from grain, distillation was also banned to ration out the precious grains for food, rather than booze.

Life in the 18th century was tough for most, riddled with hardship and poverty. While gin was not the most ideal basic need on which to spend what little money was available, it did allow those less fortunate to forget their squalor and enjoy an extremely cheap and readily available 'semi-legal' drug of choice.

the brighter side of gin ...

After the Gin Acts and the poor harvests that limited grain supply, most of the smaller-scale distillers went out of business. Gin, therefore became an expensive commodity, only accessible to the wealthy. The Gin Craze wound back, 'order' was restored and gin was produced in legitimate distilleries owned by men of good repute.

Gin was also no longer an exclusively 'London' product. The northern and southern parts of England saw large distilleries pop up, owned by wealthy families such as Boord, Currie, Booth and Gordon. Even Scotland began producing gin – a sure sign that London (and England) no longer held a monopoly on gin and gin production.

The 19th century brought further class and credibility to gin. It was more socially accepted, acknowledged by the middle class and adopted an element of bohemian approval.

Dutch gin and other imports were still considered superior to the local stuff. But, to their credit, the English producers persisted and legislators – wanting to encourage this local market – adjusted the rules again, slashing taxes on domestic spirits to make it more affordable. Now gin was cheaper than beer and, within a year, consumption doubled to over 7 million gallons. Once again, gin became affordable to the lower class but the quality diminished.

INTERIOR OF A TEMPLE OF JUNIPER.

Humbly Dedicated to its Votaries

This time round, what became known as 'gin palaces' popped up everywhere, offering what was pitched as a dazzling 'higher-class' establishment for the lower class to drink in. Much like a 'smoke-and-mirrors' scenario, the venues were considered vulgar at the time but were very popular – fitted out like expensive shops, with a shop counter, no seating and lots of low-grade booze.

This error in legislative judgement (yet again) did not go unnoticed for long, and the government removed the duty on beer to encourage patrons back into pubs and drive the price up on gin. This all but obliterated the gin palace fad – although their design did influence many aspects of later Victorian pubs (including the counter/bar and use of ornate mirrors).

By the mid-19th century, gin was peaking once again, with hundreds of distilleries opening up throughout the Netherlands, Europe and the United States. In particular, America's taste for gin during this time was largely responsible for putting gin on the global map. Embracing the Dutch genever style, as opposed to the London varieties, Americans essentially starting drinking – and making – gin because of its use in mixed drinks and cocktails. These were becoming popular in the States, and – perhaps not coincidentally – around the same time ice was becoming more readily available, which made the drinks colder (and tastier).

With the introduction of the cocktail shaker in the mid-1800s, 'mixed drinks' took on a new meaning, as did the surrounds in which they were enjoyed. Bartenders became showmen in the new-and-improved saloon bars. Their role was to keep their patrons entertained, ensuring no-one was thirsty – or left early. The longer they stayed, of course, the more they drank and the greater the dollars they spent.

the not-so-good prohibition days ...

Alcohol consumption worldwide continued to have its dark side, however, with a growing temperance movement blaming it for increased poverty and violence (particularly violence against women). Licensing hours were reduced and, by the 1920s, many local areas in Australia, New Zealand and Canada had become 'dry'. In the United States, this idea was taken to the extreme. As crazy as it seems, a nationwide ban on the importation, production, transportation and sale of alcohol – known as 'Prohibition' – was enforced across the United States from 1920 to 1933.

Also referred to as the 'noble experiment', the aim of Prohibition was to reduce crime and corruption, reduce the burden on prisons, and improve health and hygiene among Americans. Needless to say, it was a disaster.

Few can go cold turkey so easily and to impose such a ban on a whole nation would seem futile. More particularly, the reason for doing so was, in hindsight, ill-conceived. While it was seen as the logical solution to the country's violence, crime and poverty, its enforcement had a detrimental effect in the opposite direction. Crime became rampant, the court and prison systems were at breaking point, tax revenue went down while government spending went up, and corruption was rife. Dangerous substance abuse also escalated to compensate for the absence of alcohol.

Even Al Capone thrived, amassing his fortune from the illegal production and sale of alcohol, and earning notorious gangster status for himself during this Prohibition era. (See the next chapter for more on the 'bathtub gin' that was illegally produced during Prohibition.)

During this time of Prohibition, Americans turned to the somewhat mysterious and wonderful world of 'speakeasies'. These were club-style venues, designed to combine dining, drinking and entertainment under the one roof. Despite being forbidden and highly illegal, these clubs drew in both men and women, keen to enjoy the forbidden tipple (often gin) in higher-end luxurious surrounds. These venues were typically set up underground, with elaborate systems in place that would alert the patrons to conceal any sign of alcohol and boozing when the authorities were coming through. For every speakeasy shut down, another would open up, keeping the authorities on their toes and the dedicated drinkers in supply of their much-needed alcohol fix.

Once the Prohibition legislation was repealed in 1933, the demand for gin was higher than ever – more so, in fact, than in pre-Prohibition times.

The takeaway? Never take a good drop away from the mouths of grown-up babes. They get antsy.

from then to now ...

One might say (or hope) that society has become a little more rational and civilised since such outlandish times. Despite this, however, gin continued to have its peaks and troughs throughout the 20th century.

(Very) soon after the Prohibition era had moved on, gin distilleries re-emerged and it was business back again as usual. Keep in mind, the world had been through a world war (the 'war to end all wars') and a worldwide pandemic, and was in the middle of a global depression. One might suggest that there was never a better time to lift the spirits (no pun intended) than during these troubled times.

With distillation techniques vastly improved, distillers were producing a much cleaner, purer spirit, which certainly had a positive impact on the quality of gin generally and, in particular, the classic 'London Dry' gin (see the following chapter for more on this style of gin).

The surge in popularity of unsweetened, drier gin styles was also encouraged by the discovery of flavoursome and naturally sweeter botanicals such as liquorice. Undoubtedly, a better understanding of the distillation process, along with stricter regulations, was determining what should not go into gin. The darker days were certainly a distant memory and classier venues, drinks and people were now enjoying gin.

While the quality of gin was better, its popularity continued to increase and decrease through the 1900s, largely driven by new products, tastes and trends in the marketplace and, quite possibly, a desire for the youth to do things a little differently to the previous generation. With the era of cocktails, bars and then speakeasies in the 1920s and 1930s waning, for example, the world was looking for something new. In came vodka. The new Russian import, with its slick marketing campaigns, versatility and (dare I say) perceived lack of flavour, nudged gin to the side and took over the mantle as the new on-trend spirit of choice.

For quite some time, gin was highly unfashionable, and perceived as a drink suitable only for the older demographic or alcoholics. Whether gin's colourful history was responsible for this, or simply the need for change, who knows?

Despite this, gin never entirely disappeared off the radar (thanks to Gordons, Tanqueray and Beefeater), but certainly did plateau for most of the 20th century. Gin did take some time to make its comeback, but when it did, it stayed. Fortunately for us all, a new brand of gin launched in 1999 called Hendrick's helped immensely.

Pitched as a 'super-premium' gin, and infused with rose and cucumber as well as the traditional juniper, the unexpected success of Hendrick's gin was a catalyst for gin to regain its popularity, remove the stigma of its darker days, and inspire small, bespoke gin brands to join the wave of enthusiasm encouraged by gin drinkers around the world.

In 2017, gin officially outstripped vodka in popularity globally (maybe with the exception of Russia!) and interest, consumption and dedication to our beloved gin continues to surge.

Today, new distilleries, brands, flavours and quirky concoctions are launched daily. Despite offerings being vast and varied, gin is still a niche product, and standards are now exceptionally high.

If you're still reading and thinking gin could never be your tipple of choice, rest assured and persist – without a doubt, there's a gin out there for you as we delve into the different styles of gin in the next chapter.

CHAPTER 2

what is gin?

Trust me, you can dance.

GIN

By its most basic definition, gin is the combination of any alcoholic neutral spirit and juniper. In order for a spirit to be legally referred to as 'gin', juniper must be the predominant flavour and bottled (in Australia) at a minimum of 37% alcohol by volume (ABV).[2]

In fact, the only real difference between vodka and gin is the juniper.

After the juniper, further flavour is achieved with the addition of other botanicals that help develop a gin's distinct style or brand. The botanicals used are usually a combination of herbal, floral, spice, fruity, woody and earthy botanical flavours.

While all gins require juniper in order to be labelled as such, this spirit has evolved dramatically from its very early days, when (as outlined in the previous chapter) it was produced and consumed purely for medicinal purposes. Nowadays, the definition and profile of a gin is vast and varied but, nonetheless, will always have the foundation of that unmistakable aroma and intoxicating flavour derived from the juniper berry.

---

[2] Note that the minimum ABV is determined by the prevailing laws in a particular country. In the USA and UK, for example, the minimum bottle strength for gin is 37.5%.

styles of gin

In order to better understand gin, knowing about the various styles of gin you're most likely to encounter and be inspired to try is worthwhile. Different gin types often have an interesting back story as to how they came to be, and while the facts around some of these tales may raise an eyebrow, we can probably all agree that we shouldn't let the facts get in the way of a great gin story.

distilled gin

Distilled gin is considered your regular gin. Made in a traditional still, the gin is produced by redistilling neutral alcohol with juniper berry and other natural botanical flavourings. If less than 0.1 gram sweetening is used per litre of finished gin, the word 'dry' can be added to the gin or label. Apart from London Dry gins (see later in this chapter), distilled gin can have flavourings and neutral alcohol added after the distillation process, and these flavours can be natural or artificial.

genever

Not beginning this list with genever would be remiss of me. After all, this spirit is where we can attribute the magical combination of juniper and alcoholic spirit to have really begun.

As mentioned in chapter 1, 'jeneverbes' is the Dutch name for 'juniper' and it is through its use of the juniper berry that genever derived its name. It's also referred to as 'Hollands', 'jeneva', 'jenever', 'jineverbes' and 'geneva', but make no mistake – genever is genever and gin is gin. While both genever and gin have that one essential ingredient of juniper, the making of genever is made using a malt-wine spirit that may be best described as a young, unaged whisky.

Genever also typically contains less juniper flavour than gin. It is a clear to lightly coloured botanically rich spirit, with malt notes that are more reminiscent of whisky than gin, particularly because the juniper flavour is not required to be the dominant flavour, or even noticeable in the finished product. While botanicals such as angelica, coriander, orris root, ginger, nutmeg, liquorice and caraway are typically used in both genever and gin, probably the most noticeable difference between the two is the absence of citrus notes in genever.

Describing genever as a 'very compatible' marriage between whisky and gin isn't too far of a stretch, with the flavours of both combining to create something unique and, in the opinions of many, near perfect.

Similar to cognac, bourbon or champagne, genever can only be produced in certain regions. In the case of genever, these regions are Holland, Belgium and limited areas of France or Germany, as legislated by the European Union in 2008.

Genever certainly has some diversity and flexibility when it comes to drinking it. In particular, it's great to use in cocktails, with the whisky-like malt notes allowing some creative scope for recreating the old-style traditional cocktails as well as designing new contemporary drinks.

The depth and richness of flavour that comes from the whisky notes also make genever ideal to enjoy neat, on ice, with simple mixers such as ginger beer or drunk alongside beer.

london dry gin

Unlike other spirits such as cognac, tequila or scotch, a London Dry gin doesn't need to be made in a specific place or region – so it doesn't need to be made in London (or even England, for that matter). It does, however, need to be 'dry', so can't contain more than 0.1 gram of sweetening per litre.

A London Dry gin is what most people think of when they think of gin. As the name suggests, a London Dry is typically very dry with a heavy juniper flavour and aromatic notes, a botanical flavour, clear in colour and light in body.

The base spirit used must be clean, of agricultural origin (such as grain or malt) and distilled to an initial alcoholic strength of at least 96%. In other words, the base spirit must be distilled and be truly, completely neutral.

While natural plant botanicals may be included in the distillation process, the use of artificial flavourings is a no-no. All botanicals must be distilled in the neutral spirit inside the still (together or individually) or placed in a basket within the still. Apart from water, no other substance or flavouring may be added after distillation. In Australia, the gin must be bottled at a minimum of 37% ABV.

These rather stringent regulations were established by the EU in 2008 to put some clarity into the definition of what a London Dry actually is. The idea behind being super-specific with the definition of a London Dry was to maintain a high standard in London Dry production, and ensure gin isn't produced with methanol. Methanol is toxic and such standards ensure that the dodgy, backyard producer doesn't add elevated levels of methanol to increase their yield.

Rest assured, in modern-day gin production, methanol is not such an issue as any traces of methanol found are disposed of in what's known as 'the heads' during distillation. (See chapter 5 for more on this.)

Because of these regulations and modern production standards, you are assured of a quality spirit (sans methanol) that is safe to enjoy in moderation.

old tom gin

An 'Old Tom' gin is best described as a sweeter version of the classic London Dry style but drier than a genever. Its origins date back to the 1800s, when column stills (see chapter 5) weren't yet invented and the quality of gin production was at an all-time low. The base spirit used was considerably rougher – and a far cry from the clean and pure neutral spirit required by today's standards. Because gin producers could make significant profits, the less savoury distillers would add volume to their distillations by cutting their spirit with turpentine, methanol and sulphuric acid, thereby creating lots of gin that was essentially undrinkable.

In order to make an undrinkable gin palatable, sweeteners were added – anything from large amounts of naturally sweet botanicals, such as liquorice, to sugar. The roughness of the gin would determine how much sweetener was added. In doing so, producers essentially succeeded in camouflaging really crap gin.

The Old Tom style of gin was a big deal for decades. As distillation techniques – and technology – enabled improved gin production, the need for sweetening agents diminished, along with the Old Tom style of gin.

By the 1940s, the Old Tom was less in demand and, by the 1970s, had all but disappeared. As fads and trends come and go in waves, the resurgence of cocktails in 1990s enabled the Old Tom to make a comeback.

By today's standards, in comparison to a London Dry, an Old Tom will be somewhat richer in flavour, botanically sweeter, not quite as dry, but still delivering the familiar juniper punch. While it may not be the gin purist's cup of tea, it is a delicious gin style and well worth scouting out.

The preferred (or at least best known) cocktail to use an Old Tom in is a Martinez (see chapter 13).

plymouth gin

Plymouth Gin is certainly worthy of a mention in this list and – let's be honest – we must salute a gin that has stood the test of time, despite its colourful ownership history, as well as inspiring many newer-age distillers towards their own version of success.

Once upon a time a 'Plymouth gin' referred to any gin distilled in the region of Plymouth, in the south of England. However, this was halted abruptly in February 2015 and the term now refers to only one producer and brand left in the region – Plymouth. This means Plymouth Gin is both a style and a brand of gin. The company has legal protection from the European Union to produce such a gin – no-one else in the world can legally produce a Plymouth gin.

The Plymouth Gin brand was established in 1793 and, to this day, is one of the world's most recognised and respected gins on the market. It is also the oldest active British gin distillery operating in its original location, producing in a still that has not been changed for over 150 years.

Although its Original Strength version sits at a proof of 41.2%, Plymouth Gin may be described as the 'calmer cousin' of a London Dry, with a distinctly different taste. A Plymouth is less juniper-forward than a London Dry, distilled with more root botanicals to give the gin its signature earthy flavour, with subtle spicy notes.

One of Plymouth's biggest customers for many years was the Royal Navy, which was thought to purchase over 1000 barrels of Plymouth Gin a year for storing on their ships. This is where the term 'navy gin' (for gin higher in alcohol content – see the following section) is deemed to have originated from, because the gin was required to be of a higher proof (57%) to remain stable and last the distance at sea.

For a period of time during the mid-1990s, the owners at the time decided to reduce the ABV of their original Plymouth Gin to 37.5% and change the grain base to a sugarcane base. While the recipe was the same, the outcome was a gin of inferior quality and alcohol intensity which, in turn, impacted (very) unfavourably on sales. Fortunately, new ownership in the late 1990s saw the product restored to its original recipe which, eventually, boosted Plymouth back to its original status.

One of the many accolades that Plymouth Gin holds is its inclusion in 23 cocktail recipes in *The Savoy Cocktail Book*, first published in 1930. To this day, this book is arguably the coolest, most well-respected and widely used cocktail book in the world.

navy strength gin

One of my favourite gin stories centres on what we know today as 'navy strength' gin.

Back in the 18th century, the Royal Navy decreed a certain amount of gin and rum needed to be stored on board each vessel heading out to sea. The officers drank the rum and the sailors drank the gin. At the time, gin (and what was mixed with it, such as lime juice and tonic) was predominantly used for medicinal purposes to fight illnesses such as scurvy and malaria, but also delivered the added bonus of making one feel pleasantly relaxed and inebriated after having a few. When spending months out on the high seas, this was one simple pleasure that I can only assume got these men through.

Because gin was also used as a form of currency to 'pay' the men at sea, gin also held a perceived monetary value. Unlike standardised money, however, measuring the gin's quality and, therefore, its value was difficult. As a clear spirit, watering it down was easy. This diluted the flavour, but also diminished its medicinal benefits, its enjoyment and, ultimately, its value.

To prove the gin was of an acceptable standard and quality, it was tested by lighting a measure of gin with gunpowder. If it ignited and burned with a clear flame, this was 'proof' that the alcohol was of a sufficient strength and standard of at least 57%. If it didn't ignite, the spirit was below strength (known as 'underproof') and, therefore, its value to the crew was diminished. If the burning alcohol really took off with smoke and a bang, it was considered to be 'overproof'.

Around the early 19th century, the Royal Navy found a more accurate way to measure the ABV and set the required strength of alcohol supplied to them at 54.5%. Ironically, the gentleman who invented the equipment that measured the alcohol somewhere along the way determined that it should actually be 57.15%. Today, the actual minimum benchmark is 57%.

So, these days, just as gin needs juniper to qualify as a gin, a navy strength gin can only be termed as such if it is at least 114 proof, or a minimum alcohol by volume (ABV) strength of 57%. This higher strength tends to intimidate many, but a great navy strength gin is a must in any gin (or G&T) lover's collection.

While the story of its origins is certainly deemed to be true (and I'm yet to meet anyone who can confirm otherwise!), the term 'navy strength' didn't come about until the 1990s, and its use was designed to encourage the sale of higher ABV spirits. In fact, Plymouth Gin were the first to coin the 'navy strength' term when they launched their Navy Strength Gin, and this has been the benchmark of navy strength ever since.

While a navy strength gin is particularly intense and, for many, a little intimidating to drink, when it comes to making a G&T, it's the perfect gin choice. A stronger gin holds more of the essential oils from the distilled botanicals, which influences the characteristics of the gin and better communicates the flavour. When chosen as the gin in your G&T, a higher ABV will stand up to the tonic, letting the gin's flavour and notes shine through.

The same applies when it comes to choosing the right gin for cocktails. The stronger, fuller flavours from a navy strength gin won't get lost among other cocktail ingredients with strong flavour profiles.

alternative gin styles

Along with the main five options already covered, you'll likely come across a number of extra gin styles throughout your adventurous discovery of gin.

sloe gin

Despite its name, sloe gin is not technically a gin but a liqueur, originating from Britain and made with a red, berry-like fruit called sloes.

Sloes grow wild in hedgerows all over England. Harvested from the Prunus spinosa plant (a relative of the plum), they are lovely to look at but taste terrible, due to their highly astringent and overall unpleasant taste.

While the unpalatable berries aren't eaten fresh, it was discovered that they tasted incredible after being soaked in booze. Alcohol, combined with a touch of sweetener (usually sugar – added to draw out the sloe juice from the ripened fruit), allowed their lovely richness and depth of plum-like, earthy flavour, with subtle raisin notes, to develop, delivering a delicious and, generally, sweeter gin.

A good sloe gin may also carry notes of almond (almost like marzipan), which is derived from the stone of the sloe fruit.

The warmth and richness of the sloe gin was ideal for drinking in the cold UK winter, when it was ready to drink after the fruit had been harvested in autumn and macerated in time for winter.

Once the Americans got wind of the new taste sensation, they gave it a summer vibe by mixing it with citrus and soda water. The outcome? Arguably one of the most famous sloe gin cocktails – the Sloe Gin Fizz.

The origin of sloe gin can be traced back to the 17th century in England, and tends to coincide with the history of land enclosure. (Bear with me here – cool history lesson to follow.) During this time, the British Parliament passed the first of what became known as 'Enclosure Acts', which transformed what had been common land into individual properties. This subdivision of land included farms. For the land to be broken up, hedgerows were planted to establish a property owner's boundaries. These were considered more practical and cost-effective than constructed fencing,

and the natural greenery was certainly more visually appealing. And what plant was used for these hedgerows? The Prunus spinosa plant, of course!

This meant the added bonus of growing these dense hedgerows was the bountiful crop each autumn, when the sloe berries would be ready for harvest. Particularly in those times, any harvest was a good harvest and, provided it didn't kill you, it was always worth finding a way to make the most of a half decent crop. After a bit of experimentation, and the addition of alcohol, people soon discovered sloe berries could be turned from an inedible, astringent fruit into a sweet-tasting, slightly tart, ruby-red liqueur.

Sloe gin's early reputation, however, was not so great – it wasn't necessarily considered to be the best when it came to quality, and was judged a drink fit only for the lower class. It was also seen as a contributor to the 17th-century Gin Craze in London (refer to the previous chapter). However, by the 19th century, well-established distilleries had released their own sloe gins, and consumption of the beverage soon became a regular Christmas and holiday tradition.

In the early 20th century, sloe gin had another resurgence when cocktails came of age, only to peter out again mid-century. However, in more recent years, sloe gin has enjoyed a growth in popularity, largely due to the explosion of gin as again on-trend, and bartenders exploring their own creative scope to develop new cocktails with this diversified spirit.

Sloe gins tend to have a lower ABV% – anywhere from 15 to 30% is not uncommon. However, the European Union has established a 25% minimum ABV for a sloe gin to be named and labelled as such. It is also the only gin-based liqueur that can legally be referred to as a gin without the 'liqueur' addition.

The traditional way to make sloe gin is to pick the sloes when ripe (late autumn), prick each individual berry with a thorn taken from the blackthorn bush on which they grow and drop the pricked sloe berries into a glass jar of gin, with enough sugar to ensure full extraction of flavour from the sloes.

The jar must be sealed tight, flipped up and down a few times to mix the contents and stored in a cool, dark place for three months to infuse the berry flavour and colour into the gin.

In the first two weeks, the jar is turned daily, and then turned weekly for the next two and a half months.

After three months, the liqueur is strained from the sloes and stored in a clean glass jar or decanter. The aim is to be left with a clear, clean liqueur that is not cloudy.

A slightly longer steeping of the berries extracts the almond-like flavours from the stone of the fruit, which adds a lovely, distinct element of aromatic flavour in the gin.

The discarded sloes were often made into a jam or chutney, or used as a filling for liqueur chocolates.

bathtub gin

'Bathtub gin' first appeared in 1920 in the United States, and referred to any style of cheap homemade gin privately and illegally produced during the Prohibition era. During this time, gin was the most popular DIY spirit produced, and would typically be made using inferior ingredients, including cheap grain alcohol and poor-quality water, and other agents such as juniper berry juice, flavourings and glycerine.

The reference to 'bathtub' is likely due to either how the gin was stored or produced. When gin was illegally made at home, production occurred in as large a quantity as possible – while still going undetected by the authorities. The vessels used to store the gin were too big to fit under the tap in the kitchen sink and were instead filled with water from the tap of the bathtub and stored there until ready to consume.

The other thought is that the term originates from the making of the gin in metal bathtubs, which were common at the time. Not only would it have been an ideal vessel in material and size, but (unless they investigated further) authorities would have been none the wiser after seeing a clear liquid sitting in the bottom of a bath, particularly because a bathtub would not usually be considered to form part of an alcohol production line.

Make no mistake – bathtub gin back in the day was a very crude version of gin. The poor quality of the alcohol and other suspect additives was known to lead to blindness, serious illness and even death in many people. In fact, around 50,000 deaths during the Prohibition era are attributed to homemade alcohol production. It was highly unpleasant and foul to taste – hence the use of it in cocktails, where other ingredients camouflaged its horrible flavour.

Fortunately, any bathtub gins you may come across today are a playful spin on gin's colourful history. Be assured that a modern-day commercially produced gin making reference to 'bathtub gin' is not only most likely enjoyable, but safe and acceptable to drink.

pink gin

Pink gin wasn't originally a gin, but a pink cocktail made popular in England during the mid-19th century, thought to have been created by the Royal Navy in their big-buying Plymouth days. To make the gin more palatable, the dark reddish-brown Angostura bitters was added – changing the colour of the gin from a clear spirit to a diluted, pinkish colour, hence the inspiration for the name.

Traditionally, a pink gin cocktail was made up of one part Plymouth Gin, one part water, a dash of Angostura bitters and a lemon rind garnish.

Today, the spin on pink gin has gone to another level. While typically remaining a little sweeter in taste, other botanicals and fruits such as strawberries, rhubarb and cherries are now used to make a pink gin 'pink'.

Some gin purists may resent the modern-day pink gin resurgence, but others argue that new-age gins such as the pink gin can be a 'gentle' way to recruit someone across to the wonderful world of gin.

barrel-aged gin

While the concept of barrel-ageing gins may seem relatively new on retail liquor shelves, ageing gin in a barrel has been practised since the good old genever days.

More recently, barrels were used to transport and store gin in the 18th and early 19th centuries. Technological advancement eliminated the need for (and cost of) using barrels, which left wood as an alternative to modify the spirit rather than just something to store it in.

It does tend to upend many a gin purist, and is still quite unfamiliar to the newer gin enthusiast, but barrel-ageing gin does offer another element of enjoying our favourite tipple. And judging by the number of barrel-aged gins currently hitting the market, it seems safe to suggest that the spirits industry is most certainly open to enjoying barrel-aged gins.

When you think of the number of possible variations that can come from using barrels – from the wood used and the age of the barrel, to the liquid previously stored in the barrel and its origins – the combinations in barrel-aged gins and their choice of botanicals become almost endless.

Because gin is overall a lighter, more subtle spirit, it doesn't bring too many overpowering flavours to the barrel, allowing the naturally unique flavours of the barrel itself to bring some depth and diversity to the gin. What this means in practice is that gin doesn't need to spend countless months in barrels (like whisky does). As little as a few weeks will transform a gin and create some wonderful intensity, giving it many of the classic flavours traditionally found in an aged spirit.

What you can expect to find is a gin that still delivers the magic of its botanical flavours and, of course, the juniper, with the added complexity of whisky-like notes such as wood, vanilla, caramel, smoke and oak. If the producer has repurposed barrels that have aged wines or brown spirits, you can also expect the barrel-aged gin to take on some of those incredible flavours.

With an ever-expanding range of Australian and international barrel-aged gins on the market, it's well worth trying a few to see if they appeal to your palate. Likewise, it's a great way for whisky or bourbon drinkers to dabble in the lighter spirits.

The best way to enjoy a barrel-aged gin is not to treat it in the same way as a normal gin. It's not necessarily going to work as a G&T. Think of a barrel-aged gin as a sipping gin, enjoyed either neat or on the rocks. If neat's not your thing, try a quality dry ginger, which will balance out the intensity of the dominant flavours found in a barrel-aged gin.

When looking for ways to use a barrel-aged gin in cocktails, the best general rule is to swap out a rum, bourbon or whisky cocktail for a barrel-aged gin alternative. Longer, heavier-aged gins tend to complement cocktails such as a Manhattan or Old-Fashioned, with lighter, lesser-aged gins working well in an Aviation or Bees Knees.

classic versus contemporary
(and some other contenders)

Comparing contemporary to classic is like differentiating oranges from blood oranges. I tend to think of comparing these gin styles less in terms of opposition and more as telling a story about the evolution of gin and reflecting on where gin has come from and where it sits today.

It would be remiss of me not to include these styles, simply because gin has come a long way and, whether purists or gin-lovers generally like it or not, the contemporary approach to gin is here to stay.

classic gin

Typically, a classic gin is one that reflects the style traditionally produced by British distillers in the mid-late 19th century. The classic style tends to be juniper-forward in flavour and made with a neutral base spirit. In doing so, the base spirit bears minimal influence on the flavour of the gin, allowing the botanicals and juniper to define the gin's character.

The 'classic gin' style definition was identified in the 21st century around the time gin returned in popularity, due to the need to differentiate the modern gins we are seeing more and more today from the older-style gins that reflect the more traditional characteristics.

contemporary gin

Contemporary gins are best described as a classic dry gin with a modern twist. Most certainly a more recently conceptualised style of gin, the name was first coined in 2009 by the founder of Aviation Gin – Ryan Magarian. (No, not Reynolds – he came to the party later!)

A contemporary gin tends to draw the focus away from the juniper and to other botanical flavours and ingredients, such as citrus, floral or fruity notes, while still ensuring the essential juniper character remains.

Playing around in the contemporary space with gin has encouraged and inspired distillers around the world to extend their creative scope and, in many cases, be bold. By exploring new botanicals to use, adopting new production techniques and adding innovative (sometimes oddball) ingredients, the bar has certainly been raised in diversifying and modernising gin. For distillers, the 'freedom' to put a modern twist on a centuries old spirit has seen the world blessed with some amazing (and exciting) gins.

The contemporary style has also opened the door globally to drinkers – and we are certainly now spoilt for choice. It would be fair to say that contemporary gins have encouraged new gin drinkers to dabble in the gin space, particularly those who find the traditional London Dry a little overpowering and, instead, have preferred to start their gin journey with the more subtle, flavour-focused gins.

And as for the bartenders and mixologists out there, the creative juices are fast-flowing. With the popularity of cocktails resurging bigger than ever, the range of new and exciting concoctions is almost endless.

Provided contemporary gins don't step too far away from the essential ingredient of juniper – which makes gin *gin* – this new category has the ability to take gin to another (and most welcome) level.

compound gin

The 'compound' process of producing gin – where ingredients or botanicals are steeped in neutral grain spirit for a period of time – is not as commonly used as distilling. It is a more cost-effective (or cheap) way to flavour a gin, because the flavours are added without redistilling the base spirit and botanicals.

The results tend to be inconsistent, with the gin having a short-term intensity in flavour (albeit somewhat artificial) that tends to fade quickly.

gin liqueurs

While many gin purists may disagree with the inclusion of gin liqueurs in a book about gin, I feel it's worth throwing out a special mention here, particularly for newer gin enthusiasts.

Riding the massive global gin wave, both locally and around the world, gin liqueurs have emerged in the market over recent years, challenging some palates and impressing others.

Best described as a flavoured alcoholic spirit, a gin liqueur is still made through the distillation process, but the juniper notes tend to be less pronounced. Instead, other flavours such as fruits, herbs, spices, cream, flowers and nuts are infused in a gin liqueur.

Typically, these liqueurs are sweeter than gin, with a higher sugar content, and lower in alcohol by volume, sitting at around 20%. A gin liqueur is typically more viscous or syrupy, and generally not aged for too long.

Gin liqueurs are best enjoyed mixed with soda, used in cocktails or sipped straight over ice.

They may not be everyone's cup of (gin) tea, but there is certainly a growing interest and place for gin liqueurs as an easy-to-drink alternative to a gin such as a London Dry.

CHAPTER 3

the art of tasting gin

A day without gin is like ... I have no idea.

Listening to a connoisseur describe a gin can be both impressive and intimidating.

On the one hand, their ability to string together a collection of sweet, soulful words that bring a gin to life benefits from an experienced, finely tuned palate and, quite possibly, a lifetime of gin drinking. On the other hand, you might end up in the company of a gin expert who struggles to keep it simple and might as well be describing their Nanna's apple pie. After all, at times you just want to know, 'Is the gin any good?'

I've met people in the industry with barely enough 'legal' drinking years to have even had the time to develop a palate sophisticated enough to understand a gin or, at the very least, offer an accurate description of a gin's nose, mouthfeel and base notes. But then, we all know that one person with an acute palate and innate ability to decipher subtle notes and flavours that will take their appreciation of that spirit to another place.

Tasting gin is about experience. Not just the gin-drinking experience, but the occasion of enjoying a gin is an experience in itself. I remember a night out with the hubby and discovering 'the world's best bottle of red'. A dedicated weekend of visits to (almost) every bottle shop in

Victoria landed me the last few dozen left available, only to discover that the vintage wasn't too bad, but the occasion when I first drank it was much better.

The point is this – as with most things, your enjoyment and appreciation of a good gin not just about the aromas and flavours that emanate from the gin. How you drink it, who you drink it with, the glass it's in, its temperature, the level of dilution, the time of the year or even your health can all affect a gin's overall taste and experience.

Having said that, there is an art to tasting gin and those who do it well have a skillset that has taken years of experience to master. But that doesn't mean we can't appreciate the art of tasting gin and learn the basics! After all, there's nothing like a bit of practice to make something perfect.

where to start?

While gin may look the same from one bottle to the next, it's the chemistry inside the bottle that entices the senses and delivers pure pleasure. A gin is influenced by a number of factors, including (but not limited to):

- the botanicals (seasonal, fresh, dried or otherwise)
- the quantities, method of preparation, source, origin and order of distillation of the botanicals used
- the still
- the distilling method, whether pot, continuous, vapour basket, maceration or infusion
- the alcohol used, its quality and agricultural base
- the percentage of alcohol by volume (ABV)
- the level of purity of the water added
- any barrel ageing or post-distillation activity.

I cover the botanicals a little more in the following section.

botanical styles

The power and influence of the botanicals in gin can be easily underestimated. When it comes to producing a unique, well-balanced and unforgettable gin, they key is in introducing botanicals that complement each other, blend well together and don't all compete for centre stage.

As you would expect, not all botanicals are born equal. Some will typically dominate in their flavour and aroma profile, whereas other ingredients are at their best when in a supporting role, bringing out the best in the bolder, more prominent botanicals.

The botanicals used in gin are grouped into styles, based on their overall profile.

herbal

Gins with an herbal profile have leafy, herbaceous notes and are typically quite intense in flavour. Fresh or dried botanicals are used and include herbs such as basil, thyme, bay leaf, mint, rosemary and sage.

floral

Floral gins are a more recent addition to gin styles produced, and are typically more delicate, elegant and finely balanced. They're florally but, ironically, their floral notes are reflected more in the aroma rather than the flavour. (If you taste a rose petal, it doesn't necessarily taste like 'rose'.) Floral botanicals used include rose, lavender, violet, butterfly pea, chamomile and citrus blossom.

spicy

Spicy flavour profiles in gin refer to sweet or savoury spice. Sweet spices include nutmeg, cinnamon, cassia bark, ginger and cloves. Spices that fall into the savoury category include cumin, cardamom, pepper, coriander and anise. Spicy gins are often complex, with a soft, well-rounded mouthfeel.

citrus

As you would expect, the citrusy bright, zesty flavours used in gin are those most commonly associated with citrus fruits, such as lemon, orange, lime, grapefruit, yuzu and mandarin. Also included are the botanicals with citrus characters, such as lemongrass, lemon myrtle and verbena.

fruity

This covers the fruity botanicals used in gin outside the citrus family. Included are plums, berries, peach, mango, cherry and stone fruit – the list is long.

woody/earthy

These botanicals may be considered the heart and soul of a gin, and none is more worthy of a mention here than angelica root. Angelica contributes to the 'dry' in gin, with a piney, woody, earthy profile. Orris root and liquorice root are also well-used botanicals that fall into this category.

nutty

Not often included as a botanical style but more commonly used in modern, more contemporary gins, the nutty flavours deliver an exceptionally smooth finish. Think of macadamia, almond, hazelnut and wattleseed.

how to start?

When it comes to finding a gin that you best enjoy, it's hard to know where to begin. The investment can be great and, while you don't want to always 'play it safe' and might be keen to discover something new, you also want to enjoy your gin. Many gin drinkers lean towards a particular gin style and their preferred botanical ingredients. While this is usually a safe way to find a gin that suits your palate, you never know when that new favourite gin is waiting to be discovered. Make the most of any opportunity you can to attend gin tastings, and try other styles that you might not normally be drawn to. With so many new gins popping up every day, you never know when you'll discover your interpretation of the next best thing.

In order to gain the maximum benefit from a gin tasting, it's well worth the effort of setting yourself up in a suitable environment. The best way to taste and compare gins is for the gin to be at room temperature, diluted with an equal measure of water. This will highlight the qualities of a gin as well as any flaws.

When tasting a gin, try to clean the palate between sips. A sip of water (either filtered or natural mineral water) or a plain cracker will usually neutralise and reset your palate.

The way in which a gin changes on your nose mirrors the progression of aromas from the still. The most volatile notes will be your first impressions, with the heaviest notes lingering at the end.

Some further essentials to consider include the following:

- **The ideal space:** Set yourself up in a relaxed, neutral space. Tasting gin (or any spirit for that matter) does require concentration, energy and effort. Avoid smells and fumes that may interfere, such as smoke, perfumes or flowers, aromatic foods and cooking. Even an open fire can influence what you nose in the glass. A busy venue can also interrupt your thoughts and distract your mind from the task at hand.

- **The temperature:** Conduct your tasting at room temperature. The same applies for your tasting glasses, gins and water. Chilled glasses and spirit limit the release of flavours and aromas.

- **Your glassware:** The glass you choose is important. Your spirit needs space to move and breathe, but the aromas need to be retained within the glass for you to capture when you nose the gin. A tulip shaped or red wine glass with a larger bulb base works well. Make sure your glass is clean and smell the glass before pouring, to ensure no detergents or stale smells have been left behind.

- **Batching:** If sampling multiple gins, batch them up in 'like-for-like' groups. For example, lighter styles should be sampled first, London Dries grouped together and heavier, barrel-aged styles should be left to the end. Jumping from one to another only confuses your taste buds. Treat the gins with the respect they deserve.

- **Be aware of the strength:** Unless you're at the professional tasting level where blind tastings are the norm, be very aware of the ABV of any gin you taste. Gins are typically mixed and, therefore, diluted to a more manageable alcoholic strength. As covered in the previous chapter, navy strength gins sit somewhere around the 57% ABV – not many can tolerate this and it can take you by surprise, should you taste a gin without knowing its strength first. Having said that, don't be intimidated by a higher strength gin. After all, they're responsible for some of the best G&Ts you'll ever enjoy.

Sip slowly, be mindful, and learn from the experience of these tastings.

the added extras

To really get the most out of your tastings, consider these extra tips:

- Use a neutral, filtered water when diluting the spirit. Chlorinated water can have a huge impact on the essence of a gin.

- If you have a pipette handy, use this for adding water to dilute your gin samples. This facilitates consistent dilution across all tasters.

- To make the most of the tasting experience (should you be up for the challenge), take notes. A pen and journal should do the trick. Taking notes is particularly useful if you're intending to add mixers at the end, because keeping a record of which mixers worked best is a sure-fire way to repeat a positive gin drinking experience. With more mixers on offer than ever, going to the effort of writing down preferred mixers, the blended ratio and garnishes used is worthwhile.

pick your moment

The ideal time to taste is between meals, when you're developing a hunger, but not to the point of starving (if you're anything like me, you likely find it hard to concentrate when hungry). The best times are late morning (it's 5 o'clock somewhere in the world), or late afternoon. If you are peckish, this is where the water crackers (used to cleanse your palate) can help reduce the hunger distractions. You'll appreciate the tasting more when you have a clean palate, heightened senses looking for something to taste and have created time to enjoy the process.

time for you to be the judge

As mentioned, in order to make the most of your tasting experience, it's worth taking notes on each sample as you go. Logging your first impressions and other expressions of interest throughout the tasting is a great way to catalogue your thoughts and better understand the styles of gin you enjoy the most.

It's also worth tasting a gin twice – first, neat and, second, slightly diluted. (More on this at the end of the chapter.)

To get started, line up the gins you intend to taste, whether it be one or more. Limit yourself to no more than six different gins in one tasting, and do so over a period of time, to avoid crucifying (crippling) your taste buds and compromising your ability to stand up![3]

Tasting a gin involves five steps:

1. look
2. smell
3. taste
4. feel
5. finish.

---

[3] Gin tasting is not to be mistaken for gin boozing. The information in this chapter is designed to further your appreciation of gin, not teach you how to drink copious amounts in one sitting. I always encourage quality, not quantity, when it comes to drinking gin.

look

Before tasting the gin, swirl the gin around in your glass gently, giving it an opportunity to relax a little and breathe. At this point, look out for a few things:

- **Clarity:** Hold the glass to the light and check the following:
    - Is the gin bright and clear or a touch cloudy?[4]
    - Is there any sediment at the bottom of the glass?

- **Viscosity:** When you swirl the gin around the glass, what does the liquid do? Does it cling to the sides of the glass? If so, does it look oily or heavy, with long tears or 'legs' running down the glass? Are the legs long or short, thick or thin, slow or fast? For some context, the 'legs' refers to the liquid sliding down the inside of the glass. How they appear and the way they behave tells you more about the gin, as follows:
    - *Long legs:* This is an indication that the gin is high in alcohol.
    - *Fat legs:* This suggests the gin is higher in oils so the legs tend to hang, rather than fall quickly down the glass. This gin will be packed with botanicals and big on flavour.
    - *Thick legs:* The heavier legs that fall quickly are a sign that sugar has been added (not a bad thing by the way – natural sugars fall into this, and are designed to provide an overall gin flavour profile to please the drinker).
    - *Thin legs:* This indicates a lighter spirit.
    - *Skinny legs:* You've picked up the wrong glass – you're drinking vodka.

- **Colour:** All spirits are clear after distillation. Any colour in a gin (or any spirit) is developed after it has left the still. This may be achieved by either barrel ageing, macerating or infusing with other botanicals or ingredients.

---

4   The jury seems to be out on whether a cloudy gin is a good thing or not. Some higher ABV gins may have a cloudy look, particularly when water or a mixer is added. This is due to the level of essential oils held in the gin at the higher dilution, which are released when the alcohol percentage is rapidly lowered with the addition of water, ice or mixer. This cloudiness may be removed during filtration after distillation, but can also compromise on the flavour, which is in the oils. In my humble opinion, if the distiller chooses to keep the oils in the gin, they're there for a reason – to be enjoyed and to enhance the overall flavour of the gin.

smell

This is where you 'nose' the gin (I know, weird) and first discover the aromas emanating from the spirit. This exploratory part of gin tasting is where most of your tasting experience is found. It is also where you develop your first impressions of a gin.

If you think about how you approach any consumable food or beverage, you typically smell it first. Very rarely do you eat or drink anything before you smell it. The reason for this is because 80 per cent of taste is based on aroma. Aromas trigger the sensation of taste and prepare your taste buds for what's to come.

This is referred to as 'retronasal olfaction', which contributes to the flavour of a food or drink. When you eat or drink, the perception of aromas emanating from your mouth and nose contribute to the taste. Think of nosing a gin as your first introduction to its taste.

Your sense of smell is incredibly powerful and stirs up your other senses to deliver an overall sensory experience. A smell can take you back to a moment in time and help you recall an event, a flavour, or even what might appear to be an inconsequential experience (my first memory is from when I was three years old and is based purely on a smell). Amazing stuff when you think of it. So don't rush this step.

The smell step is also why tasting a gin is a more 'literal' experience than other alcohols or spirits, because the botanicals are what you are actually smelling, rather than the perceived flavours or 'vibe' from an alcohol (as may be the case in wine or whisky).

When you first nose the gin, be careful not to go in hard and fast. Doing so will anaesthetise your sense of smell. Remember that any gin you try will have a minimum ABV of 37% – three to four times the alcoholic strength of a wine.

After checking its legs, allow the gin to settle for a few moments.[5] Next, take a gentle sniff by putting your nose inside the rim of the glass. After a few extra sniffs, you'll notice different aromas coming off the gin, delivering an evolution of smells as the gin opens and breathes.

---

5   Swirling the glass immediately before nosing the gin can release ethanol notes, rather than the more delicate nuances of the botanicals.

What you'll smell is a particular order in which the botanicals feature. Firstly, the brighter, more volatile 'top notes', and then proceeding through to the 'heart notes' and finishing off with the heavier 'base notes'. Rather than a stop/start progression from one note to the next, each of these notes tends to evolve. In a sense, you're smelling the progressive story of the gin and how it's been made:

- **Top notes:** The first impressions. These notes are more volatile and tend to evaporate fairly quickly, but will transition you to the next notes. They may also be described as 'head notes' or 'first notes'.

- **Heart notes:** The essence (heart) of the gin and often the juniper, particularly if a more citrusy botanical gin. Heart notes appear as the top notes start to fade, although some top notes may be carried through to deliver a deeper, lingering aromatic experience. These may also be referred to as the 'middle notes'.

- **Base notes:** The heavier, woody/earthy botanicals that add depth and resonance. These notes typically reflect the quality of a gin by its length and finish.

If you find it difficult to detect any strong aromas, hold the base of the glass in your hands to warm up the glass and gin. Chilled gin tends to yield fewer notes and warming up the glass may help release them.

If you still get very little, don't despair. Noticing the different aromas and notes requires some practice, and also depends on the gin you're tasting – for example, it may not deliver the bold botanical flavours you were expecting. What you may experience, though, is one or more of the following:

- Notes that are herbal, citrus, spicy, floral, nutty, fruity, and/or woody.

- Notes that are quite dominant, such as juniper, which will hint at a juniper-forward gin.

- Aromas that are limited, which suggests the gin, glass or room is too cold (or you're drinking vodka).

- Your palate not being quite neutral enough to be attuned to the subtleties of the botanical notes.

taste

The fun part! Your senses are already well prepared to have an impression of how a gin might taste. If you're aware of the botanicals built into the gin, this can guide you as to what you might expect. However, some people are better at deciphering flavours than others, so don't be too hard on yourself if you don't taste what you think you should. Practice makes (near) perfect. Keep in mind also that you may not have experienced or tasted before many of the botanicals used (orris root and angelica come to mind).

Over time, you'll start to recognise the flavours that are more commonly nuanced in gin, and understand how they might behave with the varying botanical combinations.

When tasting gin, don't head straight for the gullet and throw it down. Take small sips. Your taste buds can detect five sensations only – sweet, salt, sour, bitter and savoury (umami) – and they need time to process the varying flavours, particularly when a few are present.

Hold the sample gin in your mouth. Try to press the gin with your tongue to the roof of your mouth. This will re-trigger the retronasal olfaction and encourage the maximum all-round flavour to be experienced in your mouth.

As you hold the gin, search for flavour profiles by asking the following:

- Can you taste any citrus, such as lemon, lime, orange or grapefruit?

- Are there any floral notes, such as rose or lavender?

- Is there a spice or bite to the gin, perhaps from cardamom, coriander or pepper?

- Do your senses pick up any sweetness, perhaps from liquorice root, cinnamon or nutmeg?

- Does any flavour dominate your palate, such as vanilla, rosemary or star anise?

- Does the spirit taste clean and bright or does it have any earthy, woody notes?

When it comes to taste, if you can detect a dominant botanical flavour other than the juniper, this will be the signature botanical used. With practice, you'll become more adept at recognising these flavours.

With some practice, what you should experience in your tasting is a journey from the top to the base notes. A well-crafted, well-distilled gin should be smooth when tasted neat, and give you warmth in your chest, rather than tears in your eyes.

feel

When we think of taste, we tend to revert to the flavour of something we put into our mouth. But it can also involve feel.

'Mouthfeel' refers to the physical sensations experienced in the mouth and how the senses react, or are stimulated, when you first taste the gin. The mouthfeel is distinct from how the gin actually tastes and is an important part of the gin-tasting process.

Mouthfeel is influenced by a number of things, such as the alcoholic strength and mix of botanicals used, as well as other molecular influences such as the oiliness, creaminess or even thickness of the gin. Ideally, the feel will be slightly warming and smooth, and the gin will pleasantly coat the mouth. Some gins may feel creamier, which can be influenced by the base spirit used. A burning or rough feel indicates that the gin is not entirely up to scratch. It's likely poorly made, with a few shortcuts taken (and should not be mistaken for a navy strength gin).

As mentioned in the 'Look' section, if the gin has fat legs that tend to hang, the gin is likely to be higher in oils. This also means you should experience a big mouthfeel. If the gin has thin legs, the mouthfeel will be lighter.

You'll also have a sense of whether a gin is dry (such as the London Dry style) or a touch sweeter (as you would expect in an Old Tom or even a flavoured gin).

finish

While we're now at the end of the tasting journey, this step is no less significant in assessing a gin. The finish is all-important and is where the lasting impressions are often made.

A spirit will have an aftertaste – a flavour (or flavours) that linger in your mouth. The aim is to try to recognise what those flavours might be. Does the finish leave a spicy warmth, citrusy sweetness or bitter note? Maybe you're left with an overwhelming piney or juniper flavour.

Also take note of whether the finish lingers longer or is short-lived. How long do you still experience the flavours after you've swallowed the gin? Provided the gin is good, the longer the better – not unlike the lasting impression someone makes once they've left the room.

now circle back ...

Once you've tried the gin neat, it's worth revisiting the same gin in a number of ways:

- Dilute the gin with a few drops of filtered water. This will further open up the gin and allow the botanicals to release and shine through. Take note of how the gin changes when you do this.

- Also consider (and perhaps take notes on) how the gin has further evolved with some air time in the glass.

- If you enjoy mixing your gin, choose a few of your favourite mixers to see what works best. If you love a G&T, choose three or four of your favourite tonics and mix the same gin with each tonic, starting with a 1:1 ratio. If it's too strong, increase to a 1:2 ratio by adding another measure of tonic. From here, you can work out your favourite combination and at what mix.

Once you've thoroughly road-tested a gin, you may like to move onto the next one.

If you don't find or experience all, some or even any of the styles and flavours covered here, don't despair. Persist and be patient. This process is not a natural one for many but, with practice, you will learn and understand the nuances, notes and flavours from a gin. And if you don't, who cares? What matters is that you discover new gins to love and that will provide you with that wonderful experience that comes with drinking gin.

Remember – it's about not only the gin you drink, but also the overall experience in which you enjoy that gin.

CHAPTER 4

gin lingo

Woman: I love you.
Man: Is that you or the gin talking?
Woman: It's me talking to the gin.

ANON (BUT MOST DEFINITELY A WOMAN)

When I first embarked on this crazy gin journey, at times I felt as though I had signed up for a crash course in a new dialect called 'gin speak'.

I remember nodding blankly a few too many times while talking to the expert 'gin boffins', doing my best to give the impression that I was well and truly versed in what they were trying to communicate to me.

Fortunately, when the passion is strong and enthusiasm is high, the ability to retain those learnings is a lot easier than mastering a foreign language.

Understanding a few of the technical terms around gin tends to fuel a desire to learn more. It also builds a foundation of understanding around the nuances of gin, particularly when it comes to tasting, mixing and even purchasing a gin that's just right for you.

You will notice that some of these terms have already been mentioned in the earlier chapters in this book, and others will pop up through the rest of the book as your gin journey continues.

If nothing else, the following will provide you with some background knowledge, and an appreciation and understanding around this awesome spirit – enough at least to converse with a fellow gin boffin.

general gin terms

When you first come to tasting and buying gin, a basic knowledge of the following can come in handy:

- **ABV:** The abbreviation for 'alcohol by volume', this is a measure of alcoholic strength and shown as a percentage. The higher the number, the stronger the alcohol. The ABV of water is 0% and pure alcohol is 100%. If 100ml of spirit is 40% ABV, this means there is 40ml of 100% alcohol in that 100ml measure. In Australia, the minimum ABV for gin is 37% and a navy strength gin must have a minimum ABV of 57%. Most gins have an ABV of 40 to 43%.

- **Base spirit:** The neutral alcoholic spirit (and an essential ingredient) used to make gin. Think of it as a blank canvas for producing a gin, where botanicals are added in the distillation process to create a unique gin spirit.

- **Blended gin:** A gin made by distilling each of the botanicals individually and then blending the distillates together in the required proportions to produce the end gin product.

- **Botanical cuts:** Also referred to as 'cuts', this is the process where the first and last part of a distillation (the heads and tails) are separated or 'cut' from the body of the distillation (the hearts). Taking cuts removes the undesirables in a distillation that unfavourably affect the quality of the gin. It also removes the toxic alcohol methanol. (This process is described in more detail in chapter 5 but, rest assured, when you're drinking a commercially produced gin, it has been made by a distiller who is well trained to know when to 'cut'.)

- **Charge:** The alcohol placed into the body of the pot still. In the case of a pot distillation, the charge includes the base spirit alcohol and botanicals. For vapour distillation, this refers to some or none of the botanicals, depending on the vapour distilling process used (see later in this list).

- **Classic gin:** A gin made with a neutral base spirit that reflects the traditional, juniper-forward flavour typical of the British dry gins produced in the mid-19th century and 20th century. The style category was identified in the early 2000s, when newer contemporary gins emerged. This led to the need to differentiate the original traditional style from the newer ones.

- **Cold compound gin:** This gin style is flavoured with essences, extracts and/or by infusion or maceration without distillation. These gins are considered of a lower standard to distilled gins.

- **Compound gin:** A gin made by steeping juniper berry, botanicals or other ingredients in a neutral base spirit for a period of time. Think of vodka steeped with botanicals – that's a compound gin.

- **Contemporary gin:** A modern-style gin that redirects the focus away from the traditional piney juniper flavour and towards the flavours of the other botanicals, such as the citrus, spice or floral. Juniper is still an essential ingredient, but not necessarily as prominent. While many a gin lover tends to move away from these gins, the contemporary styles have proven to be a successful gateway for the new gin drinker to adapt to – and appreciate – this awesome spirit.

- **Distillate:** The liquid produced through distillation.

- **Ethanol:** This is the alcohol base of a spirit. Also referred to as ethyl alcohol, drinking alcohol, pure alcohol or neutral spirit, it is a colourless and flammable liquid. Ethanol is an essential ingredient for producing spirits.

- **Fixatives:** A gin's character and aroma is best experienced when you first open a bottle of gin. These escaping aromas may fade over time, reducing a gin's complexity, flavour and aroma. A fixative performs the function of stabilising a gin, enabling it to maintain its consistency over time. Some of the more commonly used fixatives are coriander seed, nutmeg, angelica and orris root.

- **Grain to glass:** The 'paddock to plate' for gin. A gin that has been produced from scratch by its maker will involve the growing of the base spirit's raw material (for example, grain, grape or corn), mashing, fermenting and producing the base spirit and then further distilling the base with botanicals to produce the end product – gin.

- **Louching:** The response when a clear spirit turns cloudy or opaque. This occurs when a spirit contains hydrophobic essential oils that are soluble in alcohol, but insoluble in water. Over time, the cloudiness tends to dissipate but, regardless, it doesn't affect the quality or flavour of the gin. In fact, the opacity is a reflection of the flavours extracted from the botanicals.

- **Maceration:** This involves soaking botanicals in a base spirit for a period of time prior to distillation. Macerating botanicals helps draw out the essential oils so they are easily captured during distillation. Alternatively, maceration (also known as 'infusion') can take place after distillation where botanicals are added to the distillate to further flavour a gin.

- **NGS:** The abbreviation for 'neutral grain spirit'. Most base spirits are made from grain (hence the 'grain'). The NGS usually sits at around 92 to 95% ABV.

- **Proof:** A measure of alcohol percentage. The term dates back to 16th century England and was used as a basic measure of alcohol content, initially for rum and, eventually, for other spirits. If a spirit is 40% ABV, it's classed as 80 proof (in the US).

- **Rectification:** The process of running an alcoholic spirit through a still. This is done to clean up a spirit by removing impurities, concentrate a spirit to a higher proof ABV or flavour a spirit by redistilling it with botanicals.

- **Vapour/botanical basket:** A perforated basket used to hold botanicals in a still for distillation.

- **Vapour distillation:** The placing of botanicals in a basket, rather than directly into the pot still. When the still is heated, the alcohol boils and converts into vapour, which rises through the botanical basket. As the vapour passes through, it gradually extracts the flavours and aromas over the distillation period. The benefit in doing so is to preserve the integrity of the botanicals – so that botanicals aren't prematurely stewed or cooked in the heated alcohol. The order botanicals are placed in the basket can dramatically affect the gin's flavour, with the flavours more easily extracted from the botanicals on top rather than those underneath.

- **Yellow gin:** A gin that has been stored in a wood barrel. The reference to yellow comes from the subtle colour change of the gin as a result of the contact time spent in the barrel. More commonly referred to as a barrel-aged gin today, the term 'yellow gin' was coined from the way gin was stored on ships back in the 19th century.

taste

Some terms that relate specifically to taste include the following:

- **Bottom notes:** The heavier end notes that follow the heart notes and typically reflect the quality of a gin by its length and finish.

- **Finish:** This describes the way a gin fades away from the palate. The finish may include:
  - the flavour that lingers for the moments after sipping and how long it lasts
  - the enduring sensation – whether the alcohol causes heat or a burning sensation, or is smooth or rough
  - the astringency (dryness) in the mouth
  - the bitterness from tannins, particularly in barrel-aged gins.

- **Flavour profile:** This describes the flavour and aroma of a gin. Various flavour profile categories have developed over time that enable most gins to be catalogued into one or more categories. The most common flavour profiles are citrus, herbal, spicy, floral and juniper-forward.

- **Heart notes:** The middle part (notes) of a gin's flavour profile. Heart notes transition from the top notes and reflect the essence, or body, of the gin.

- **Juniper-forward:** Juniper is an essential ingredient in all gins. In a London Dry gin, juniper technically must be the dominant flavour. 'Juniper-forward' is the term used to describe a gin that predominantly has that juniper flavour that gin junkies love, and is the first taste you'll experience in a juniper-forward gin. A strong, juniper-forward gin will taste almost like the berries have been picked straight off the tree and placed into your mouth. A really strong juniper-forward gin experience will taste like you're sitting in the tree chewing on the berries!

- **Mouthfeel:** The way the gin feels (not tastes) in the mouth. This refers to the various sensations and textures experienced when the gin touches the palate, including the tongue, roof of the mouth, throat and even teeth.

- **Nose:** The smell or aroma of a gin – your first impressions when you smell the gin.

- **Palate:** The taste of a gin.

- **Terroir:** A reflection of how a gin might capture the character of a specific geographical area through the botanicals used in a gin or, in the case of a base spirit, the origin of the raw agricultural materials used. For example, a distillery in a wine region may use a base spirit made from local grapes, or may use a local indigenous botanical as the key ingredient.

- **Top notes:** The initial aromas and your first impressions. Also referred to as 'head' or 'first' notes.

drinks

Drinking gin also involves some key terms:

- **Dirty:** A martini with added olive brine.

- **Dry:** A less-sweet gin drink. In the case of a martini, less vermouth is added to make the drink less sweet.

- **Neat:** A drink served without ice or mixer.

- **On the rocks:** A drink served in a glass with ice.

- **Straight up:** A drink served without ice or mixer in the glass, but shaken or stirred first with ice, then strained and served in a chilled glass.

- **Twist:** If you order a drink 'with a twist', you'll find a twist of citrus peel in your glass. More often than not, expect lemon.

For more on mixing gin-based drinks, see the chapters in part IV.

PART II

DELVING INTO ALL THE PARTS THAT MAKE THE WHOLE

CHAPTER 5

how gin is made

Chemically speaking, gin is a solution.

The most challenging part of bringing this book to life was writing this chapter well, to ensure I not only covered the many facets of gin production (and pay homage to those creative talents who produce this exquisite drop), but also write it in such a way that could be easily understood and, at the same time, allows the craft behind the production of gin to be appreciated.

Why?

Because making gin is not just a 'one size fits all' process. It's a carefully configured, well-polished and finely tuned craft that relies on following intricate systems with the level of care necessary to get it right, while also accepting the need for flexibility throughout the process and knowing when to do so.

Gin is a science. It relies on attention to detail, a deeper level of thought and consideration, fine precision and good timing. A tailored process needs to be followed to ensure that the end product is as close to 100 per cent consistent every time.

Gin is also a work of art – so much so that no two gins are exactly the same. One might even suggest that no two batches of the same gin are identical, particularly when it comes to making smaller batch, artisanal craft gins, using botanicals that can change with the seasons and be easily influenced by natural processes beyond human control. Even the same gin recipe produced on a different still can be remarkably different.

And that's the beauty of gin.

Think about the production of wine, where each season's grape harvest is so heavily influenced by Mother Nature – the climate, the season, the sun and rain, the time of harvest and the winemaker's skills. No two vintages will ever be quite the same.

The same can be said for gin. Consider the juniper berry – where flavour is influenced by the time of harvesting, its growing season and the length of travel from all corners of the globe. Then there's the base spirit for the gin. Is it a grain, sugarcane, grape or corn base? These base ingredients all rely on climate, health and time of harvest, all of which can be sometimes unpredictable.

Next, take a look at the botanicals. The flavours from these can be influenced by whether they are fresh or dried, new or aged, and by the quality of the season, at what stage and in what order they are introduced throughout distillation, infusion or maceration, and how they blend with their botanical companions.

Spirits can be produced in many ways, from the very rough to highly refined. In the case of gin, a few essential steps must be taken, not the least of which is to have a recipe to follow and a handful of vital, non-negotiable ingredients. Even when it comes to the recipe, however, a lot of this creative process is down to trial and error.

As for any artisan in their field, the procedures and processes detailed in this chapter are not a cookie-cutter, 'one size fits all' method for making gin. Consider the work of the distiller to be not unlike that of a professional chef. Respect the art, the individual's techniques, skillset and – above all – passion for their craft.

The following processes describe the production of gin, although most of these same principles are also applied in the production of other spirits, such as vodka, rum, whisky and brandy.

the steps

The steps in gin production can be summed up in three steps:

1. producing the base spirit
2. distilling with botanicals
3. finishing the product.

While this process might appear relatively straightforward, it's never quite that simple, but it is fascinating. To provide a clear and detailed picture, I start at the very beginning, so you can not only appreciate the level of effort and attention to detail required to make a great gin, but also become an armchair expert as to how it's done.

Firstly, gin needs a few essential ingredients:

- a neutral/base spirit
- juniper
- botanicals
- water (only good stuff).

producing the base spirit

To produce a base spirit, the steps covered include:

- sourcing the ingredients
- making a mash
- fermenting the mash
- first distillation.

the ingredients

All gin starts with a base spirit – also referred to as ethanol. To produce a base spirit, you need a number of essential ingredients:

- A raw agricultural ingredient that contains sugar or starch, such as grain (wheat, barley, rye or corn), grapes, sugar cane, potatoes, whey, quinoa or even apples. The only criterion – by law – is that the base alcohol must be of agricultural origin. Grain is more commonly used, particularly for gin, because a grain-based spirit tends to give gin a crisper texture. This is not to discount in any way the level of quality in a base spirit produced from other sources. In fact, some of the world's best gins use other raw ingredients for their base spirit.

- Yeast, which is used in the fermenting process to convert the raw ingredients into sugars that, in turn, produce alcohol. The process of fermentation is remarkably simple – the yeast feeds off the sugars. In doing so, two products are produced – ethyl alcohol (ethanol) and carbon dioxide.

- Water – as good and as clean as possible. For some brands, the water is where the brand story begins and is deemed the key ingredient to producing a quality spirit.

making a mash

The ingredients are used to make what's called a 'mash'. Water is heated and the crushed raw ingredients are added and mixed together to create this porridge-like mixture. The mash is where starches are transformed into sugars, through the addition of yeast and a resting period known as fermentation.

fermenting the mash

The fermentation process is where the alcohol is created. For fermentation to take place, two things are needed – a raw material in liquid form that contains sugar (that is, the mash) and yeast.

The process of fermenting has been around for thousands of years, and anything containing sugar can essentially be fermented and converted into alcohol. Keep in mind, though, that not all alcohols produced through fermentation are fit for human consumption, so don't try this at home (and, besides, it's illegal to do so).

Fermentation typically takes around one to two weeks and is regularly monitored along the way to determine when the fermenting process is complete. This is determined when the percentage of alcohol (also known as alcohol by volume – ABV) has reached its peak. This is usually around 7 to 10% ABV and is achieved when the yeasts consume all of the sugars present in the mash.

The finished product is referred to as the 'wash'. At this point, the wash is ready for its first distillation, which extracts the alcohols to produce a base spirit known as the neutral alcohol or ethanol.

first distillation

This is the process where the alcohol is extracted from the wash. For every 100 litres of wash, roughly 10 litres of ethyl alcohol (ethanol) will be extracted through the first distillation process. This means the ethanol extracted is a highly concentrated, purified and polished neutral spirit with an ABV somewhere around 95%.

It's important to keep in mind that distillation doesn't actually create the alcohol, but merely concentrates it. In other words, fermentation is the process that 'makes' alcohol, and distillation cleans and condenses it.

The first distillation is achieved by boiling the mash to separate the ethanol from the remaining unwanted alcoholic, non-alcoholic and chemical congeners. Because ethanol boils at a lower temperature (around 78.2° Celsius) than water and at a different temperature to other alcohols, extraction is possible during distillation.

To explain this in everyday terms, think about what happens when you take a shower. The hot water that rises up as steam and hits the mirror (a cold surface), recondenses back into a liquid in the form of droplets. That's distillation.

While the aim of this first distillation is to achieve a clean, neutral and unflavoured spirit, don't assume it plays no role in the final outcome of the spirit (in this case, gin) produced.

The raw ingredients used, along with where, how and the season in which they're grown, the fermentation, first distillation and level of purity all contribute in some subtle way towards providing a quality (or not) base spirit.

In the case of gin, the base spirit is the starting point to producing a high-quality, delicious gin. The base influences the mouthfeel, the smoothness and other subtle nuances that, when further distilled with the juniper and other botanicals, will add depth and value to the overall flavour profile, aroma and quality of the end product.

Consider a good base spirit to be a strong supporting act for an exquisite gin.

distilling with botanicals

Once the base spirit is ready, the next step is to start bringing the essential ingredients together to make gin. This is done through a further distillation, where the following takes place:

- adding the juniper and botanicals

- separating the heads, hearts and tails

- getting it right.

This point, for many commercial distillers, is where the production of gin begins. The vast majority of gin producers begin with ethanol produced by a third party that can guarantee the quality and consistency of the neutral base spirit. This is important to ensure that the end product in the bottle is consistent in every batch produced. The other issue is the cost of producing a neutral spirit, as well as the space, time, efficiency, resources, equipment – and sanity – required. All play a role in why a distiller does or doesn't produce their own base spirit.

If you're moving into gin geeks and freaks territory (and, yes, most of us are), please remember that starting the production of a spirit from grain to glass is not easy or cheap, or even valued by most. That's not to say those who do produce their own base for gin are wasting their time – in fact, quite the opposite. Likewise, a distiller who starts at this point still requires skills, patience and passion to produce a quality spirit.

It's important to appreciate that there are many different ways to get a lovely gin to the bottle and, no matter at what stage a producer begins, it's never easy to do.

adding the juniper and botanicals

This is also the point where the botanicals used to flavour gin and the alcohol come together. Of course, as with all gins, juniper is the main ingredient, alongside the botanicals that a distiller chooses to create his or her unique gin blend. This is where the botanicals used, the order in which they're added and the precision of heat and speed of distillation and timing all come into play. It's also where the distiller's skills, passion, instinct and craftsmanship play a role in the production of a beautiful spirit that makes people happy. (For more on the botanicals used, see chapters 6 and 7.)

heads, hearts and tails

The distilling process has three stages – the beginning, the middle and the end, also known as the heads, hearts and tails.

heads

The heads (also known as 'foreshots' or 'congeners') are the more volatile – and less desirable – elements that are removed in the early stages of distillation from the distilled spirit. The heads are not only highly unpleasant in taste and smell, but in some quantity can be quite toxic (I'm pointing the finger here at acetone and methanol[6]). Fortunately, these congeners have a lower boiling point to the ethanol, so their extraction at the beginning of distillation is a standard – and safe – process.

In some cases, a miniscule amount of the heads may be deliberately included in the hearts in order to provide some complexity and depth to the hearts of the spirit. This is where the talents and expertise of the distiller comes into play.

---

6   Methanol is toxic and should not be consumed. Consuming methanol can cause an array of health issues, including blindness and even death.

As the temperature continues to climb in the distillation process and the heads have been successfully extracted, the hearts are next to follow. This is the sweet spot in the distilling process and the stage where the gin you drink comes from. The hearts give you the clean taste that the distiller is looking for and contain the smoothest, beautiful botanical-flavoured gin.

hearts

The distiller's objective is to collect as much of the hearts as possible, without contaminating it with heads and tails. This is why the early part of distillation requires patience and must not be rushed.

In order not to miss any of the hearts being discarded with the heads, because this reduces the liquid volume of flavoured ethanol spirit (in this case, gin) extracted through the distillation run, a distiller takes careful note in these early stages to ensure that the heads are 'cut' at the right time – just as the hearts start to follow through.

This decision is made in a number of ways. For ease of understanding here, this is predominantly through smell and taste, and one of the telltale signs is when the solvent smell of acetone disappears and the sweeter, smoother smell and taste of ethanol emerges. However, an experienced distiller will also instinctively know when this cut should be done, because the transition out of heads into hearts (and from hearts to tails) is a gradual one. This means the decision often comes down to the distiller's experience and their passion for the product and process. Knowing when to make good cuts can be the difference between a cheap spirit that delivers a hangover the morning after and a top-shelf product.

For the visual thinker, when the distiller 'cuts' from heads to hearts, the flow of the distillate (the spirit) is moved from one container to another.

tails

The tails (or 'faints') is the final stage in the distillation run.

Once again, a distiller's patience, considered decision-making and experience determines when the extraction of the hearts has come to an end and the next cut needs to be made to separate the precious hearts from the toxic tails.

Identifying when hearts end and the tails begin is largely based on sight, taste and smell:

- Firstly, an oily film from the botanicals will appear in the distillate. This is a sign that the tails are flowing through.

- Secondly, the flavour profile of the hearts will dramatically change. The desired botanical flavours and pleasant aromas will start to fade and the sweetness of the ethanol spirit will diminish.

- Thirdly, the smell of the tails will emerge. This smell is described in many ways, all of which are unmistakable – from old socks and shoes, to wet dog, to cut grass left with the deposit from that same wet dog.

From a more technical perspective, by this stage in the distillation, the alcohols with lower boiling points have evaporated and what's left are undesirable alcohols and other unwanted compounds. They are highly unpleasant to taste and, should they contaminate the hearts, may have a detrimental impact on the quality of that production run.

When the timing is right, the distiller will divert the flow of the distilled spirit to another container to collect the tails. Once the distiller has collected the hearts and it is evident the tails are following through, the intricate part of the distiller's job is done.

In gin production, the tails are a big no-no. Having tasted them once before (and most certainly will never do so again), I know firsthand the tails are the dregs of the distilling process, where the heavier oils from the botanicals and other undesirables collect. You can safely assume that the world's best mixer won't redeem the tails.

getting it right

Anyone who thinks the job of a distiller is simple has never distilled – or at least never distilled well.

The mark of a great distiller is in knowing when to cut the heads and the tails, with the aim to collect as much of the precious hearts as possible. Cutting too early or late may contaminate the hearts at either end. Likewise, cutting too late or early may mean that the optimal quantity of the hearts is caught up in the heads and tails. Either scenario can mean the delivery of a poorer, more inconsistent spirit quality, as well as diminished quantity – all of which has a huge impact on the dollars and cents for the producer. (Put simply, less hearts = less dollars.)

The art of precision is key. As mentioned, a distiller will often make the call on whether a touch of heads should be included to improve the character of a spirit. If this is the case, then consistency is key, for the consumer has an expectation that every bottle purchased is going to taste the same every time.

The required cut of a distillery's house brand may also differ from the distiller's own interpretation or preference as to where that cut should be – and this is why you might discover a 'distiller's cut' gin. Keep in mind that no-one on the planet has a monopoly on what is good, great or excellent – that decision rests with you, the gin drinker.

The art in gin distillation is also why we are so fortunate to have an ever-expanding range of gins to choose from. In the case of my fellow gin lovers, there's never been a better time to explore the diversity of botanicals and flavours now found in gin, whether that diversity be dictated by geographical location, botanicals used, distilling techniques or even distiller's cuts – and that's before you've added the mixers.

the final cut – finishing the product

At this point, the gin has been made, most of the hard yards are complete and just a few final steps are required to take this magnificent drop off the production and into the bottle.

Four main steps are left:

1. infusion or maceration
2. dilution
3. resting
4. bottling.

infusion or maceration

Infusion or maceration can actually take place prior to distillation or for a period of time after. Infusion is the simple process of steeping botanicals, such as herbs, spices, fruits or nuts, in a base spirit, allowing the alcohol to draw out the desired flavours and aromas and preserve them in the alcoholic spirit. Maceration is a similar process, but instead of steeping the botanicals are broken or opened up to allow the alcohol to more deeply penetrate the botanicals to extract a richer flavour.

The idea behind macerating is to bring out the best features of a particular botanical, particularly when looking for a balance between the more dominant botanicals that are incorporated into a gin. This process is popular when producing a more contemporary, flavoured gin with different complexities and unique flavour profiles. If you find a gin that is coloured, chances are its botanicals have been macerated after distillation.

Infusing or macerating may take a few hours, days or even weeks, depending on the speed of extraction, the botanicals macerated and the desired flavour being drawn out. The key is to not over-extract, so the process requires an understanding of not only the botanicals being used, but also how they behave in the alcoholic liquid.

Think of this in terms of your favourite cup of tea, which uses the infusion method. Leaving your tea leaves to infuse for too long releases a bitterness that makes the taste of the tea highly unpleasant. On the other hand, not steeping some teas for long enough means the right balance of flavour isn't released. The same ideas apply to gin and the botanicals.

dilution

The gin distillate typically measures somewhere around 92 to 95% ABV. This needs to be diluted down to the required proof (at least 37% ABV in Australia). Water is gradually added to the distillate – not the other way around – and stirred constantly to ensure successful blending.

The water needs to be as neutral in flavour as possible, devoid of any excessive minerals or hardening substances and clean and clear. As it's being added, the mix needs to be stirred constantly to ensure successful blending and minimise any haziness.

resting

No hard and fast rule exists as to how long gin should rest prior to bottling. Some distillers rest the distillate for days, others for weeks. It's also not uncommon for gin to be bottled first and then rest.

bottling

Once blended, the gin is ready for bottling and labelling – and, finally, to be enjoyed.

still types

Two main types of stills are commonly used for distillation – the pot still and column (or continuous) still.

pot still

A pot still (also known as an alembic still) is the traditional still used for spirits production. While still popular and well used, these types struggle to produce large volumes as efficiently as a column still. Pot distillation operates in batches, rather than continuously. Today, they're more commonly used for flavour-rich spirits such as whisky and brandy, because of the heavier, richer alcohol that can be distilled to create interesting flavours in the spirit once matured.

Despite their limited capacity and efficiency, pot stills come with a sense of tradition, with some distillers believing they produce a spirit of quality and character.

A pot still has a main chamber (the pot) that is heated up, boiling the contents. At varying boiling points, the contents produce steam vapour that collects in a second chamber called the head. The vapour caught here is directed towards a tube known as the 'swan neck'. The vapour continues on to a condenser, which cools the vapours, converting them back into a liquid so they can be captured.

column (continuous) still

The original column still, invented in the late 1820s, was a brilliant innovation for the distillation industry. However, while the first models impressed in their appearance, they lacked in their ability to produce a half-decent spirit.

This changed in 1830 thanks to the Irish inventor Aeneas Coffey, whose modifications to the continuous column still meant a much cleaner, purer spirit was produced. Drinkers could say goodbye to the dangerously poor quality, turpentine-tainted, even sawdust-infused gin that was available at the time. Fortunately, the modern-day gin lover never needed to experience such a travesty.

The column still has the ability to continuously produce large quantities of spirit 24/7. A handful of the world's biggest brands will run their stills non-stop for up to a year or more, without needing to shut down the still for cleaning or servicing.

With the column still producing a smoother, more purified spirit, the need to camouflage the taste of the gin was no longer necessary – and the need for added sugars was significantly reduced (and eventually removed entirely).

A column still works by a steady flow of the base spirit (or wash) being fed into a column. With the use of steam, the compounds are vaporised through a series of plates (or trays) that are evenly spaced up the column. Each plate is slightly cooler than the plate below.

As the vapours hit the plates, condensation starts to form. With hot vapours constantly flowing through the system, the condensed vapours repeatedly drop back down and are redistilled over and over back into a vapour state, making contact with the plates each time to further purify the spirit. This constant redistillation from vapour to liquid to vapour separates the heavier compounds (the less desirables) from the lighter compounds (the good stuff!), all the while cleaning and purifying the spirit.

Once the distiller is satisfied with the level of purity of the spirit, she or he will draw the condensed liquid from the still – the hearts.

Column stills must be monitored constantly by the distiller and can be the difference between a good and great gin.

The inclusion of a vapour basket containing the botanicals suspended in the still allows for flavour extraction as the ethanol vapour rises through the basket and botanicals. This tends to deliver a softer flavour and can be used exclusively or in conjunction with the maceration of the botanicals.

making the perfect gin

As you can appreciate, making gin is in no way straightforward. Much of the process is trial and error, learning about botanicals and how they behave, and understanding how they interact with their companion botanicals.

Patience, timing and passion are incredibly important. Accepting the distilling process is a slow and steady one that must not be rushed is key to producing a world-class gin.

Choosing botanicals that complement each other, understanding how they each perform on their own and as companions, working out their ideal ratios and when and how to introduce them, and knowing when you've stumbled on to the flavours, notes and aromas you've been looking for, can be a painstaking process – best described as an intricate work of art.

Some gins take years to create; others have been found in the first run.

Regardless, when a producer reveals their gin to the wider world, there's a sense of trepidation, fear and excitement all at once.

One thing is for certain, though, there is a perfect gin out there for everyone.

CHAPTER 6

it's all about the juniper …

I love water ... especially when it's frozen and surrounded by gin.

I am often asked what makes our own Heathcote Gin different from all the other gins out there. Depending on who's asking, I've been known to respond by comparing the creation of a gin to making chocolate cake.

A chocolate cake can be made in quite literally thousands of different ways, with recipes created for generations throughout different cultures, designed by some of the world's best chefs or written ad-hoc in hand-me-down cookbooks. But while there are countless variations in the ingredients list, preparation and cooking techniques, they all essentially have one common ingredient – chocolate (of course).

The same can be said for gin. A unique and (almost always) delicious gin can be created in limitless ways, but gin has one essential ingredient it cannot do without – the juniper berry.

In fact, without juniper berry, gin cannot be legally classified as gin.

Juniper is what gives gin that familiar 'piney' taste. The combination of how that gin is produced, its origin and the other botanicals included is not unlike a gin having its own DNA. Line up a dozen clear-spirited London Dry Gins and you'll no doubt be blown away by how different one gin is to the next, despite them all looking exactly the same. That's the beauty of this incredible spirit – and has, without a doubt, played a role in generating so much interest in this fine spirit on a global scale.

what is juniper?

While it's named and referred to as a berry, the juniper berry is not actually a fruit but the female seed cone of the juniper tree – a short to medium-height evergreen conifer tree from the cypress family. The actual juniper berry is best likened in size, shape and colour to a small blueberry, and was traditionally used as a culinary herb or spice. Its strong piney smell and bitter, citrusy taste contradicts its fruit-like appearance and while it's certainly edible on its own, juniper is best used as a fragrant savoury ingredient in cooking and, of course, in drinks.

The berries are round in shape, with an unusually fleshy texture and fine scale-like appearance on their outer coating. They grow all year round and collect in clusters on the branches of the juniper plant.

The berries are green when young, maturing to their purply blue–black colour when ripe – a process that takes around 18 months for most species. Their flavour and aroma are at a peak immediately after harvest, gradually declining in intensity over time.

horticulturally speaking ...

Juniper plants thrive in the wild and, once established, require little maintenance. They enjoy dry, sunny growing conditions in mountainous forest and desert areas. Over 50 species of juniper are found in most countries in the Northern Hemisphere, growing to varying heights.

Once established, juniper shrubs are drought tolerant and non-deciduous and, due to their evergreen appearance, are versatile in the garden or wider landscape. Because of their smaller size and shape, with foliage sitting close to the ground, they're effective in weed management as a groundcover, help to prevent soil erosion and survive well in sub-standard soil conditions.

Common Juniper is found growing in varying elevations and climates, from the English and Scotland Highlands, through to Iceland and coastal Greenland, Alaska, Canada and Northern USA, and throughout Europe, Japan and Northern Asia.

Once established, the plant requires very little maintenance or pruning – just a regular harvest of its precious berry.

The young green berries have a dominant flavour and aroma of 'pinene', which is best described as a resinous, woody pine note. As they mature, and their green colour ripens to the darker blue-black colour, their resinous character delivers green-fresh, citrus notes. Inside each juniper berry is approximately six hard, black seeds. This is where the flavour is found.

The outer scaly skin has minimal flavour which, when used as a spice, is typically crushed before use. When used for gin, the juniper berries are usually dried. Once the dried berries are added to a distillation, the alcohol will effectively permeate through the outer skin to draw out the all-important juniper flavours.

Now here's where it gets really quirky. Juniper is 'dioecious'. What this means is that, unlike most tree species, where male and female flowers grow on the same tree, the juniper plants are either male or female, not both. When the male flowers appear in the spring, their yellow flowers release pollen, which is carried in the wind to pollinate the flowers on female juniper plants. The female flowers appear as minute clusters of scales. Once pollinated, they grow into the green, berry-like cones. These then mature and ripen into dark purply blue-black scaled berries, and are ready for harvesting in about 18 months.

It's not unusual to find a juniper shrub with its berries in different stages of maturation, with green and ripe berries covering the tree at the same time.

Once planted, a juniper plant typically takes two years (and two winters of dormancy) to establish themselves before berry production begins. While they are slow growing, once established, they will be prolific in their berry offering and, provided the shrub is planted in ideal conditions, will prove to be a resilient and low-maintenance plant.

Juniper trees can survive for many, many years – even centuries. Some of the oldest trees in the world are found in places such as Macedonia (where a large portion of the juniper berry used by Australian distilleries comes from), and these are over 400 years old.

juniper's humble origins ...

The history books attribute the discovery of juniper berries and their early uses to the Greeks, who used it for its medicinal value long before its value was found in food and beverages. The Greeks also believed juniper berries enhanced physical stamina and used them as a supplement to boost the performance of their Olympic athletes.

The juniper berry was also used by other ancient cultures for varying perceived benefits. The Egyptians used the juniper berry to cure tapeworm and embalm the dead, and in the time of the Roman Empire, the berries were used for purification, managing stomach ailments and as a cheap substitute for the prohibitively expensive black pepper (how times have changed!).

In central Europe, juniper berry was considered a remedy for the 'poorer' disorders, such as cholera, dysentery, tapeworm and typhoid, while in Canada, juniper was used to treat tuberculosis, rheumatism, ulcers and topical wounds.

The wood of the juniper was deemed limited in its value, but considered useful for its highly aromatic smoke, used for ritual purification of temples. It was also thought to open up contact with the otherworld and a reliable 'path' for clairvoyants.

Alcohol was traditionally used to preserve the medicinal value of juniper berry, while also providing a pleasant side effect of making one feel more 'relaxed' after consuming the alcohol. As mentioned in chapter 1, this encouraged an era of hypochondriacs, who enjoyed the perceived cure for their apparent ailments.

other uses of juniper

While most people typically draw the connection between juniper and gin, the berry has traditionally been used as a spice for cooking in many cultures. Northern European and Scandinavian cuisines often feature juniper berries in their dishes, particularly when cooking game meats (such as boar, venison and game birds), as well as a seasoning for pork, sauerkraut and cabbage dishes. Northern Italian cuisine has traditionally made good use of juniper berries to flavour brines.

any health benefits?

Just to be absolutely, abundantly and categorically clear, my medical knowledge here is very much limited to Dr Google. The benefits of juniper berry pre-distillation are also different from those post-distillation when making gin. Despite this, some of the more interesting uses and perceived health benefits of juniper are worth sharing, if for no other reason than to pump this little dynamo's awesomeness.

Like most berries, they're a good source of vitamin C and antioxidants, and are known to have anti-inflammatory properties. Juniper is still used in a limited capacity today for the treatment of digestive and intestinal irritations, gastrointestinal and urinary tract infections, as well as relieving heartburn bloating and stones. Other recorded uses include the treatment of snakebites and skin wounds, managing joint and muscle pain, and the treatment of bronchitis, asthma, arthritis and sciatica. How effective – or dubious – these treatments are is questionable and the efficacy for these conditions is somewhat unproven.

As an essential oil, juniper is used in aromatherapy and perfumery, deemed to have useful antiseptic properties and known to aid digestion and relieve flatulence. Juniper is also considered to have a diuretic benefit by increasing urine production. (Note: this does not include when caused by an over-enthusiastic consumption of gin!)

While most juniper species are edible, some are not. In fact, some are highly toxic and poisonous. The common juniper species (Juniperus communis) is the most frequently grown, harvested and used juniper species for culinary use and gin production.

Eating the leaves of the juniper tree will make you ill, and eating the root of the juniper is highly toxic.

The research behind the use of juniper berries beyond their value in cuisine and beverages is somewhat limited. However, it is definitely not recommended for children and should be avoided by women who are pregnant.

does juniper grow in australia?

The short answer is, 'Yes, juniper can grow in Australia' but, in fact, very few juniper shrubs or trees are actually grown successfully in Australia. The reason for this is simply because our climate isn't suitable for growing juniper in enough abundance to support our own Australian gin industry.

We do, however, have our own indigenous juniper known as boobialla (also known as coastal boobialla or Myoporum insulare). It is a hardy native that has adapted to our often harsh growing conditions, and can be found growing wild on dunes, along cliffs and in sandy soils across most Australian regions, including Western Australia, South Australia, Victoria, Tasmania and New South Wales. It is a fast-growing, salt-tolerant plant, that fruits annually towards the end of summer.

Boobialla produces a small white flower in the warmer months, with its dark purple fruit following soon after, and usually ready to harvest at the summer's end. The fruit of the boobialla bears some resemblance to the Juniperus communis, with similar juniper-berry like qualities in both flavour and aroma. It grows to approximately 1 cm in diameter and has a lovely bright purple colour when ripe and ready for harvesting.

Boobialla juniper has been used in a small number of Australian craft gins and, with some luck, will continue to feature more prominently in years to come.[7]

---

7   The very well regarded and talented duo Sarah and Jon Lark of Kangaroo Island Spirits have successfully planted and grown their own common juniper trees and used this juniper in their own gin production.

the wonder of juniper

Without a doubt, the juniper berry warrants a chapter of its own, if only to outline some of its rich history and help you appreciate its value and influence in our world today.

The magic of juniper is in its transformation from a small, seeded cone to producing one of the most celebrated beverages in the world. The all-too familiar intoxicating perfume of earthy pine, with an intricate palate that covers woody, spicy, peppery, citrusy, mentholy mint-fresh greenness, is quite unlike any other, and the flavour that it delivers, is the signature note of any good, quality gin.

CHAPTER 7

the best of the
botanicals

I'm on the gin and tonic diet ...
so far I've lost 3 days.

Gin has certainly come a long way, and the evolution and modernisation of gin has elevated this wonderful imbibe to now hold the mantel of one of the bestselling spirits in the world. And while gin lovers adore the piney juniper flavour that personifies gin, we simply cannot underestimate the power of the other botanicals and ingredients that also deliver excellence to the world's greatest spirit.

The influence of botanicals plays a significant role in building a gin's DNA and, therefore, their importance cannot be underestimated. In fact, botanicals enable gin lovers around the world to be gifted with what appears to be an almost endless variety in their preferred tipple. This variety and specialisation not only showcases the creative brilliance of distillers and producers around the world, but also tells a tale about a gin's country of origin and the story behind its humble beginnings.

The use of botanicals in gin has never been more exciting, diverse, daring and, in some cases, downright crazy.

In 2014, Cambridge Distillery in the UK launched Anty Gin, using red wood ants. Soon after, in 2017 Australia was blessed with the launch of the incredible Australian Green Ant Gin from Seven Seasons.

Portobello Road has suspended an organic turkey breast over its still to produce the Pechuga Gin, and a motor cycle enthusiast thought it might be a good idea to steep gin with engine parts salvaged from an old Harley Davidson motorbike (nice and niched!).

You may already be familiar with the use of cannabis in gin, which comes with the promise of momentous joy and euphoria. Even collagen has laid its claim to fame in a bottle of gin.

The one that interests (but not necessarily entices) me the most is the gin that combines the scent of freshly unwrapped Egyptian mummies and gin (yes, you read that correctly), using botanicals traditionally used in the ancient Egyptian embalming process.

In modern-day gin production, the botanicals often play a key role in the gin story, providing the gin with a 'sense' or 'expression' of place, and connecting that particular gin with an origin to tell its own story.

how the botanicals are used

In simple terms, the process of adding botanicals typically takes place in the distillation stage of gin making, where the essential oils and aromatic compounds from the botanicals are absorbed by the neutral spirit in which the botanicals are steeped or, alternatively, as the vapours pass through the botanicals (usually through a vapour basket).

Different flavours and essential oils are drawn out of the botanicals at different temperatures during distillation.

Botanical flavours can also be added to a spirit by macerating botanicals after distillation. Depending on the botanicals macerated after the distilling event, this may produce a coloured gin, rather than a pure clear spirit.

The key is finding the balance in the raw botanical materials used, ensuring they complement their fellow botanical mates in the gin recipe, and wisely selecting the quantities of each to ensure a desired – and truly delicious – outcome. The distillation time and quality of the 'cut' (see chapter 5) is also crucial to bringing out the best of the gin and its botanicals.

botanical styles

Bringing botanicals together to make a great gin is an art form in itself. While a range of botanicals are harmoniously well-matched, the gin maker's talent and background knowledge, along with a touch of common sense, logic and creative scope, play a role in producing a uniquely delicious, unforgettable gin.

Keeping in mind that all gins must include juniper as a key botanical, botanicals tend to fall under a particular style. This is useful when learning about gin and, more particularly, discovering what's best suited to your personal gin palate.

The main styles, and the botanical options within them, include:

- Herbal: Basil, bay leaf, mint, eucalyptus, peppermint, lemon balm, angelica root, rosemary and sage.

- Floral: Rose, lavender, butterfly pea, chamomile, hibiscus, jasmine, elderflower, geranium, honey and orris root.

- Spicy: Coriander seeds, cardamom, anise, cinnamon, cassia bark, ginger, nutmeg, star anise, pepperberry, cumin, chilli pepper, pink pepper and river mint.

- Fruity/citrusy: Raspberry, strawberry, lemon myrtle, citrus, finger limes, bush tomato, plums, berries, lilly pilly and rhubarb.

In chapter 3, I also highlight citrus, woody/earthy and nutty botanical styles separately (and in their own right).

the stocky standards

While quite literally thousands of raw materials can be used to produce gin, a specific range of botanicals are more commonly used and, in some cases, relied upon. To be honest, the 'shortlist' of commonly used botanicals was more manageable a decade ago, but some tried, tested and essential botanicals still feature in most gins produced around the world today.

Their inclusion in gin not only provides some familiarity (or diversity) in a gin's flavour profile, but may also perform the function of providing stability to the gin itself.

Included here are some of the most widely used gin botanicals in the world. Of these, four are used more than any other, commonly referred to as the 'fab four'.

the 'fab four' combo

You'd be hard pressed to find many gins that don't include the 'fab four' botanicals – coriander seed, a root (usually angelica root), a citrus and (of course) juniper.

juniper

Juniper is worthy of a chapter all of its own. You can find everything you need to know about this incredible botanical in chapter 6.

angelica root

The function of angelica root should not be underestimated when it comes to making gin. Angelica is like the mother of all botanicals, holding it all together to ensure the volatile flavours of other botanicals remain stable and marry well, providing length and substance to a gin.

Angelica offers earthy notes to a gin's flavour profile, best described as woody, nutty, damp and root-like with a piney edge. Distillers tend to look for smooth, mellow qualities when choosing their preferred source of angelica root, because some regions produce a more pungent product, which will affect a gin's outcome. Fortunately, the quality of the root is not dictated by its place of origin.

The seed of the angelica plant is also used (but less commonly) as a botanical in gin, delivering celery-like, slightly floral fragrant notes.

Angelica is believed to have originated from Belgium, but has traces back to Syria. It grows wild throughout Europe and is cultivated in Germany, France, Romania as well as some East Asian countries. It is not uncommon to find it growing wild in Australia, in backyard gardens or even prolifically on the side of the road.

All parts of the angelica plant are well used throughout culinary traditions. The stalks can be eaten as a vegetable or even candied, but only the seeds and roots are used when distilling gin.

coriander seed

Next to juniper, coriander seed is the most commonly used botanical and, therefore, plays a prominent role in gin production. While the distinct flavour of coriander does divide public opinion (due to a genetic predisposition in a quarter of the population, who taste soap when they eat coriander leaves), coriander seed is undoubtedly the near-perfect essential ingredient when it comes to making gin.

The seeds are small, round and light tan in colour. They have a bright, high-toned citrusy spice, and a sometimes nutty and often floral quality to them that brings body, intensity and complexity to a gin.

Coriander's origins have been connected to Italy, but history also tells a story of its oldest archaeological find being in Israel. Having said this, Tutankhamen had it stored in his tomb, and the Greeks were cultivating coriander as early as the second millennium BC.

Sourcing coriander seed is a big deal for distillers, because its growing location impacts heavily on the overall flavour profile. How it is prepared before distilling will also influence a gin's outcome, with the seeds roasted, crushed or kept whole.

Putting on my boffin hat for a moment, on a molecular level coriander seed oil is made up of a single alcohol called linalool and alpha-pinene, the key ingredient in juniper. So coriander and juniper blending as well as they do makes sense, complementing each other to bring out that wonderful flavour that makes gin, gin.

The flavour of coriander seed tends to be discernible somewhere near the end of your palate's flavour journey when tasting a gin. If a gin has citrusy botanicals, these are likely to feature towards the beginning, with the citrus notes from the coriander seed presenting themselves towards the end (heart) of the gin.

citrus

The next of the 'fab four' botanicals used in gin is the citrus family – and the options here are vast, including orange, lemon, lime, grapefruit, mandarin, tangerine, cumquat, yuzu and bergamot, as well as their related varieties and cultivars.

When referring to citrus as a gin botanical, typically the citrus peel is used, but including the entire fruit is not uncommon. The peel contains a higher proportion of the fruit's flavoursome oils, which carries (and holds) well in the alcoholic spirit.

Citrus peel is a familiar flavour in gin and adds brightness to the overall profile. Gin makers often focus on these bright, refreshing and sweeter notes because they lift and complement other botanicals included in a gin.

Lemon and orange are the most used from the citrus family. As you'd expect, distilled lemon is distinctly lemony in flavour and aroma. The amount used will determine its level of dominance in a gin, and using the peel will deliver a different outcome compared to using the fruit of the lemon.

Oranges used in a gin can dramatically affect a gin's flavour. While we typically enjoy a sweeter orange when eaten as a fruit, the more bitter varietals (such as the Seville) are more commonly used in gin, because the rind carries more oils and imparts a more compatible flavour.

The earliest records of citrus originate in China, dating back over 4000 years. Citrus plantings reached Europe and northern Africa 2000 years later, and they are still grown abundantly in these regions today. Nowadays, citrus grows almost anywhere. In Australia, we are blessed with some of the best citrus varietals in the world.

the best of the rest

As already mentioned, the botanical possibilities with gin making are almost endless. Here's just a small handful of the most commonly used today in gin.

cardamom

Cardamom is a warm, highly aromatic spice native to Southern India and commonly used in Indian and Middle Eastern cuisine. Guatemala, however, is the largest producer and exporter of cardamom in the world and, in some parts of this region, the crop is considered more valuable than coffee.

Originating from the same botanical family as ginger and turmeric, cardamom is one of the most expensive spices in the world. It's also one of the most complex and difficult to describe other than it tasting and smelling just like … well, cardamom. Some people also note a piney flavour as being part of its complexity – making cardamom another spice that marries well with juniper.

The cardamom plant grows from two to six metres in height. The fruit is harvested, cleaned and dried. The fruit resembles a small three-sided oval pod that contains small, hard, brownish-black seeds. This is where the flavour is found.

Cardamom is most commonly used as a pod that's then crushed to extract the flavour from the seeds, or pulverised into a powder form.

While widely used as a botanical in gin, only a small amount of cardamom is needed to impart the benefits of its strong, aromatic character. The botanical value cardamom provides is a distinctly sweet, spicy flavour that blends particularly well with juniper and coriander.

cubeb berries

A member of the pepper family, the cubeb berry adds a complex mix of peppery allspice, aromatic lemon and eucalyptus and piney notes to a gin.

Typically found growing in Indonesia, cubeb trees are often planted among coffee plantations. The fruit berries are small in size, harvested by hand when they are still green (before they fully ripen) and carefully dried, which changes their colour from a ruddy-brown to greyish-black.

liquorice root

Liquorice root is a somewhat naturally sweeter botanical, traditionally used in Old Tom style gins to mask the taste of the poorer quality base spirit used to make a substandard gin.

Originating from India and southern Europe (and, would you believe, from the pea and bean family), liquorice root creates a sweeter flavour profile in gin, but with the added benefit of a fresh, bittersweet, woody-earthy taste. While liquorice is similar in flavour to anise, aniseed and fennel, they are not related at all botanically. You may also be surprised to know that liquorice root contains a compound called glycyrrhizin, which is up to 50 times sweeter than sugar.

Liquorice root adds length and depth, a touch of sweet and the ability to soften and round off a gin.

anise

Anise (also known as aniseed), is a large flowering plant native to Southwest Asia and the Mediterranean. Anise is almost identical in flavour to star anise, but a lot more expensive to grow.

Anise delivers a similar flavour to liquorice, but with mild basil notes.

grains of paradise

One of the world's most famous gins – Bombay Sapphire – includes this botanical. Native to and grown in West Africa, grains of paradise delivers warm and peppery overtones in gin, imparting a flavour reminiscent of pepper, cardamom and coriander.

orris root

I love sharing with gin lovers the origin of this botanical. For me, orris root is one botanical that really highlights how closely gin is connected to Mother Nature.

Orris root is actually the bulb of the iris flower. The bulb itself is a prolific multiplier when planted, but its transition from flowering bulb to gin botanical is a significantly more arduous process.

Traditionally, orris root is better known for its use in perfumery. Similar to its use in gin, orris is a base note used by some of the world's best known brands, including Chanel and Yves St Laurent. Along with its contribution to the scent profile, orris was also used in perfumery for its properties as a fixative, stabilising fragrances, aromas and flavours with a missing atom. Without the addition of orris root, the fragrant properties from other botanical ingredients were volatile, unstable and easily lost.

The ability for orris root to perform such a function stems from the length of time required to bring orris root to its prime. The process begins when the plants are developed for three to five years to reach ideal maturity, both in size and age. The bulbs are then harvested, peeled and left to dry out for up to five years.

This drying time allows the flavour to develop and the fixative properties to become effective. This finished product is a very hard bulb, which is then finely chopped or ground into a powder to maximise its value.

Orris root is also a widely used culinary spice, particularly in Middle Eastern and Moroccan cuisine – think ras el hanout, and you have the essence of orris root.

When it comes to gin, orris root's primary function is again to stabilise the other botanicals, utilising its fixative properties. What this means in terms of gin production is that the orris root tightly binds to other aromatic botanicals to reduce volatility and provide stability in the overall balance of a gin.

Orris also provides a range of notes to a gin. The actual root has a distinct smell of violets but, in essence, the notes that feature in gin are earthy and woody, with a hint of floral sweetness.

cinnamon

Cinnamon is a diverse ingredient, crossing the boundaries of sweet, savoury and spicy, making it incredibly versatile in the culinary sense. When it comes to its botanical value in gin, cinnamon tends to complement the sweeter notes by delivering a fiery, spicy edge.

Like cassia, cinnamon is also sourced from the bark of a tree – in this case, one that's native to Sri Lanka called the *Cinnamomum verum*. Cinnamon is harvested all year round by peeling away the outer bark of the tree to access the softer, inner layer. As the bark dries, it naturally curls into a tightly coiled, multi-layered quill.

The cinnamon quills are softer than cassia and easier to break down or grind. Cinnamon is more commonly used in powder form domestically but distillers typically use the cinnamon sticks when making gin.

cassia bark

The evergreen cassia tree originates from the south China region and is a close relative of cinnamon. Predominantly grown in China, Vietnam and Madagascar, cassia is produced by harvesting the bark from the tree and drying it into quill rolls that very closely resemble (and can be mistaken for) a cinnamon stick. Upon closer inspection, the cassia is thicker, single-layered and harder to break down or grind.

Unlike cinnamon, cassia emits a fiery scent, with an earthy tone and sweeter finish, reminiscent of liquorice. Its subtle oily sweetness, with some spice and complexity, adds a little warmth to the flavour profile. A familiar botanical found in gin, it's typically used only sparingly.

As a botanical, cassia tends to bring a sense of familiarity to what you'd expect to taste in gin, probably because many gins include this as a key botanical. Cassia adds complexity to a gin that manifests warmth, earth and spice flavours.

appreciating the world of botanicals

This botanical list is in no way even close to being an exhaustive one. Countless botanicals are available to us – many of which are yet to be discovered, and all of which we can credit to Mother Nature.

In Australia alone, over 6,500 indigenous native botanicals are available, and the gin world hasn't even scratched the surface of working its way through these, let alone the countless other botanicals available in all corners of the globe.

So please enjoy the journey of exploring the new, the unique and yet-to-be-discovered wonderful world of botanicals. If I hope anything can be achieved through the writing of this book, it's that I manage to open your eyes to better understand and appreciate the truly incredible botanical offering. We are fortunate to be able to explore – and enjoy – these through the spirit of gin.

CHAPTER 8

choosing your ideal mixer

The role of a good mixer is to be the bridesmaid to the gin bride.

THURMAN WISE, DIRECTOR OF BRAND AND INNOVATION, CAPI

It doesn't seem that long ago that choosing a suitable mixer for your gin was an easy decision to make. If you're a more 'established' gin drinker, you'll no doubt remember a time when Schweppes was the go-to tonic for your G&T, and premium artisan brands simply did not exist. Soda water barely got a sideways glimpse and heaven forbid a dry ginger would even make it to the list of options.

While it seems a lifetime ago that we were limited with the offerings, it's only been in the past decade or so that some of the mixer biggest brands in the world have been born. What is clear, though, is that we are now spoilt for choice, with almost as many mixers on the market as there are gins. This means choosing a mixer is no easy task. And just because one mixer tastes delicious on its own, you're not guaranteed it will pair well with your favourite gin.

Fortunately for the lovers of gin, it's this vast offering that provides some added interest and diversity to the gin-drinking experience. Finding your perfect pairing, understanding how the flavours, aromas and botanicals behave, and attuning your palate to what you best enjoy makes the gin journey even more fun.

Like choosing a gin, no hard and fast rules exist as to what you should mix gin with. After all, your taste buds are your own and no book can tell you what you 'should' enjoy. Your preferred style of gin and how it is ideally mixed, garnished and served is entirely up to you. The decision as to what works best lies completely with you and your palate.

Having said that, you need to keep in mind that the mixer can make up the majority of the drink in your glass. It's also worth remembering that the role of the mixer is to be a strong supporting act to the star of the show – your gin. You want to avoid the two competing for centre stage on your palate. The two should meld together as though they were made for each other – a perfect match made in gin heaven.

It's also important to remember that a mixer doesn't need to dominate your glass in volume. Depending on the gin and mixer you choose, work on a more even ratio of gin:mixer to begin with – going as low as a 1:2 (or even 1:1) ratio is a good place to start, gradually adding more until you find the ideal blend for you.

You may be surprised how much mixer you don't need in your glass. After many years of drinking a G&T, I've heard of people 'discovering' gin for the first time when reducing their gin:mixer ratios.

tonic water

Gin and tonic have (almost) been together forever. One's the ying to the other's yang. It's arguably the most popular mixed drink on the planet and has a distinct taste quite unlike any other.

Despite this, many people simply despise the bitterness of the tonic or, at the very least, don't enjoy a G&T. If this is you, don't despair. Not only is there a gin out there for everyone, there's also a tonic out there now for every gin (and gin drinker).

Fortunately, with the range of brands and flavours available today, the tonic no longer needs to be a mortal enemy, but instead can be your new best friend.

Schweppes have been serving its Indian Tonic Water since 1870 (and supporting G&T drinkers ever since), but the newer premium brands have certainly helped fuel the latest gin boom in many ways:

- With the arrival of Fever-Tree in 2005, the market experienced a dramatic change in the way we perceive not only the flavour of tonic water, but also its premium value.
- Fentimans, the company that brought us the world's first botanically brewed mixers, set the bar high for brands to find innovative ways to deliver a 'supporting act' product into the spotlight, encouraging others that would ultimately follow.
- Our local lovely CAPI brought quality and class to the mix (no pun intended) with an ever-expanding range of 100 per cent natural, preservative-free mixers.
- Strangelove – another local favourite – is an Australian brand conceived by childhood friends, with a goal to be different and a vision to change the way we approach our gin. With a focus on local ingredients and unique, eclectic flavours, their range certainly leaves you spoilt for choice.

Supporting and enjoying local products is a drum I love to beat, and it's easy to do with the vast range of gins and mixers available on your doorstep (no matter where you are in the world).

Try this …

When you're in the Friday night 'gin o'clock' zone, get four glasses, one gin and four different tonics, and try this:

- Pour one 10 ml nip of your selected gin into each glass.
- Add 10 ml of each tonic to a glass.

You now have four variations of a G&T with the one gin.

Try each of them, and then ask yourself the following:

- Are they too strong? If so, add another 10 ml of the tonic.
- Do they pair well? If so, they're on your short list.
- Does one stand out or a few?

And remember – if you're still in doubt, choose your favourite tonic.

choosing a tonic

So how do you choose a tonic for your gin?

To be completely frank, there's no straightforward answer. Back in the day when the choices of gin and tonic were few, the options were simple and, despite the lack of diversity and quality available, our palates were in no position to complain.

Nowadays, the combinations are endless and there is most definitely no right or wrong answer. Remember, it's all about what you respond favourably to. Drinking your best friend's favourite drink is pointless.

The challenge – and fun – is in exploring what's available and finding your own perfect mix. Here are some tips to guide you:

- Again, a good mixer is one that doesn't try to take centre stage in your glass. A good mixer lets the gin shine through.

- An 'old school' mixer, such as Schweppes, pairs well with the more traditional gins, such as Bombay, Gordon's and Beefeater.

- Don't flood your glass with tonic. You'll be amazed at the difference and balance in flavour when you gradually add the mixer to your gin in the search for your ideal balance.

- Despite the bitterness of tonic, don't be fooled – it is a sweet drink that contains sugar and, in some cases, lots of it. Fortunately, a good number of low-sugar tonics are now on the market that are delicious. They can also make space for the nuances of your gin to shine through.

- Just as we don't encourage the 'busy shirt, busy tie' look, for a bolder gin, choose a reliable all-rounder craft tonic that doesn't try to compete with the gin's botanicals.

other mixer choices

If the tonic is just not your thing, other options are available for you to choose from.

soda water

Soda water is bubbles in its simplest form. It's the perfect accompaniment if you just can't get that tonic taste to oblige your taste buds, and is a healthier, sugar-free option (if that's an important factor in your decision to drink gin).

If the subtle saltiness in soda water is a challenge, opt for a natural mineral water instead.

sonic

A more recent, and increasingly popular alternative to tonic or soda water is to blend the two, creating a gin & sonic. This tones down the intensity of the tonic flavour, dials back the sugar and makes space for the gin to sing its song.

ginger ale

I love a good dry ginger ale and, with the ambitious, new-age gins on the market, a great number of them pair beautifully with the ginger bite.

To pair with ginger ale, look for gins featuring smoky flavours, chilli, rhubarb or fruity gins, or orange-based gins. Think in terms of cooking and what flavours go with ginger – if you find those botanicals in a gin, pairing it with ginger ale is worth a try.

ginger beer

If you're thinking ginger beer is virtually the same as ginger ale, think again. Ginger beer typically has a much stronger flavour, with real ginger bite and a little more intensity than its dry ginger cousin. Having said that, both can be used in a similar way and with a similar style gin, but the measured quantity used may differ from one to the other.

Using my taste testing method, you can switch out a tonic for a ginger beer when testing what pairs best with your chosen gin.

soft drinks

(Gin purists – don't shoot me down here. We're recruiting …)

I find that many new gin drinkers who struggle with the piney, woody notes of the gin and the quinine of the tonic find the gentle transition into appreciating gin comes through adding a mainstream mixer, such as lemonade, lemon soda or even cola. Keep in mind that less is more, and it's always easier to add more mixer rather than subtract.

Enjoy your exploration through the ever-expanding catalogue of mixers. Particularly when you're investing in a good bottle of gin, don't penny-pinch on the mixer. While I'm a firm believer that a good gin needs to be a standout on its own, finding the ideal mixers will only further enhance your gin experience.

CHAPTER 9

the finishing touches – your garnish guide

Charles Dickens: A martini, please.
Bartender: Olive or twist?

I'm frequently asked what garnish goes with what gin. To be perfectly honest, sometimes taking the time to find a suitable garnish just gets in the way of enjoying a gin, and I'm a firm believer that a great gin should not need to rely on a garnish to make it palatable. Similar to the mixer, a garnish should be seen as a strong supporting act that further enhances the joy of drinking gin.

Having said that, the power of the garnish cannot be underestimated. Particularly with some of the more dominant flavours, such as star anise or vanilla, the garnish can make or break a perfectly good gin – and a well-chosen garnish can redeem a gin that's not a flying favourite.

A garnish is also a magnificent finishing touch. Presentation is everything and taking the time to design and build a beautiful cocktail or beverage is as important as the actual drinking experience. After all, it's not just about the drink, but the experience that aligns with the occasion.

Getting a little creative in choosing your garnish ingredients and being meticulous in your preparation and proud of your final presentation can make a great drink even better.

choosing a garnish

When choosing a garnish, remember that the role of the garnish is to further enhance your gin experience. It does this in a number of ways:

- accentuating a botanical flavour already in the gin
- adding a new flavour that complements the gin's botanicals
- providing balance and harmony within the flavours
- making your G&T or cocktail look (and taste) delicious
- done well, providing a complete, memorable sensory experience.

While there's no hard and fast rule when it comes to choosing the perfect garnish, it is possible to miss the mark. Having said that, pairing your gin to a suitable garnish is all down to personal taste, so don't be limited by what's deemed acceptable. Instead, learn to trust your own palate.

Garnishes usually work best when they complement the gin style you're drinking. The following lists some common styles and the garnishes that work with them:

- **Dry:** Generally suits orange, lime, lemon, grapefruit, olive, juniper berry and citrus peel
- **Citrusy:** Works well with citrus (lemon, lime, orange), fresh coriander, basil, mint, thyme or rosemary, coriander and star anise
- **Fruity:** Pairs well with chilli, berries, basil, pomegranate and peppercorns
- **Floral:** Tends to suit edible flowers, apple, berries, grapefruit, rosemary, rhubarb, lavender, cucumber, rose petals and citrus (or its peel)
- **Herbaceous:** Works with rosemary, thyme, apple and peppercorns
- **Spicy:** Compatible with peppercorns, ginger, star anise, cinnamon stick, orange or lime peel, chilli and capsicum (bell peppers)
- **Sweet:** Try with berries (fresh or frozen), citrus, apple, rosemary or basil, and edible flowers
- **Savoury:** Garnish with fresh rosemary, thyme or basil, peppercorns, olives or even a cherry tomato.

To avoid ruining a perfectly good tipple (or to redeem a not-so-good one), here are some useful guidelines that make the process of deciphering what goes with what a little less daunting:

- Match your garnish to a signature botanical featured in your gin. The idea is to draw out that botanical flavour. For example, if orange is a botanical used in the gin, garnishing with orange will highlight that lovely citrusy botanical flavour.

- If you have a favourite botanical, use that as your garnish. When you have an affinity to a flavour that you enjoy, it may be the ideal addition to complement your gin.

- Look in your garden, pantry or fridge. You just might have the ideal garnish readily available that's not typically used or considered and, if close at hand in the backyard or kitchen, chances are you enjoy its flavour. Peppercorns, basil, thyme, chilli, or cinnamon stick are all worth experimenting with.

- Don't be afraid to play around the edges. Be bold and creative and look for unexpected pairings. The person who came up with the idea to pair chilli and chocolate, for example, or strawberry and basil was a genius.

- Don't be limited to one garnish for each gin. Any one gin will most likely work well with many garnishes, and cross over varying gin styles.

Try this …

Experiment with one gin across three garnishes to find what works for you:

- Pour a standard 30 ml shot of gin across three glasses (10 ml in each glass)
- Add a different smaller-size garnish to each 10 ml shot
- Let each one sit for a moment and then try them.

Write down in your journal (if that's your thing) your favourite garnishes with a particular gin. Alternatively, write it on the back of the bottle's label.

The seasons may affect the flavours of your garnish which, in turn, may have an impact, either favourably or unfavourably, on a particular gin. Herbs in season taste significantly better than they do at the tail end of their seasonal cycle. Likewise, it's hard to find a better flavour than a berry in its prime.

Remember that your palate also changes, sometimes from one day to the next. Your health generally can also tamper with your taste buds.

And keep in mind it's not just about the taste or flavour. Also take in the aromas, texture of the garnish, and mouthfeel of the gin with a garnish.

Above all, do not think that every gin needs to be garnished. A good quality gin should be able to well and truly stand on its own. The addition of a garnish should either further enhance the gin's essential qualities or, at least, create a pleasant, alternate drinking experience with the gin.

Most importantly, and as always, what someone else likes you may not. No-one has a monopoly on what is right when it comes to taste and personal preference.

Try this …

Put a spin on garnishing your gin, G&T or cocktail with the following:

- Boil a few herbs in water for a few minutes.
- Drain and cool, and then freeze in water in an ice cube tray.
- Use the cubes as a substitute in an herbaceous gin with your favourite tonic.
- Garnish with the same or complementary herb.

You'll notice the flavour of your G&T will evolve throughout your drink. (You can also try this with berries, citrus or even spices frozen in ice cubes.)

dehydrated garnishes ...

There's a lot of interest at the moment around dehydrating your own garnishes. They are a delicious alternative with a well-paired gin, and they allow you to extend the life of a seasonal garnish, such as blood orange, by preserving the fruit and boosting the intensity of its flavour, through dehydration.

A number of good, great, exceptional – and expensive – options are on the market. While they're pretty reliable in delivering you a near-perfect dehydrated garnish, you can also achieve a great result in your oven.

Dehydration is one of the most ancient methods of preserving foods, having been discovered many thousands of years ago. Back then, it was done to ensure food security. Now, it's done to save one's gin-sanity!

The natural (and most cost-effective) way to dehydrate foods is in the sun. However, with this method you have to rely on two things:

1. a dry climate with temperatures reaching 30°+ C

2. the birds or other animals (including the neighbour's cat) not swooping in and taking them away.

The further downside is that this process can take two to six days, depending on the weather and the thickness of your garnish slices. The upside is that if you do succeed, you'll have flavoursome, dehydrated fruit garnishes that can only serve to improve your gin drink.

The significantly quicker, but slightly costlier, process is to dry your garnishes in the oven. Here's how:

1. Preheat the oven to 70 to 90° Celsius, using the fan-forced option if you have it.

2. Wash and dry the fruit thoroughly.

3. For pitted fruit, remove the seed before slicing.

4. Cut the fruit into thin, even slices so they dry out over the same time period.

5. Spread the slices flat on a tray lined with baking paper, making sure the slices don't touch. If space permits, fill up two to three trays to be economical with your oven.

6. Check and flip each slice periodically. (While this is a fairly low-maintenance, low-supervision process, you do need to check the slices to ensure they're not burning, and flip each slice to ensure they dry evenly.)

7. If you don't have a fan-forced oven, open the oven door regularly to let the excess moisture out.

This process will take a few hours – typically anywhere from six to ten hours, depending on the fruit, the thickness of the slices and its juiciness.

The best fruits to dehydrate in the oven include:

- **The citruses:** Orange, lemon, lime, grapefruit and cumquat
- **Stone fruits:** Cherries, nectarines, plums, apricots and peaches
- **Seed fruits:** Apples and pears
- **The unexpected ones:** Bananas, strawberries, raspberries, blueberries, pineapple and kiwi.

Once you've found the ideal pairings for some of your favourite gins, take advantage of the garnish for some visual appeal. When beautifully balanced and executed well, the visual impact may very well turn a lovely drink into a truly memorable gin experience.

PART III
BUILDING YOUR BAR SKILLS

CHAPTER 10

mastering mixology

The problem with the world is that everyone
is a few drinks behind.

HUMPHREY BOGART

Mixologists and bartenders today require a range of skills that extend well beyond knowing how to mix a good G&T. Gone are the days when even the stock standard cocktail fare was enough to keep the clientele entertained.

Natural flair and a touch of theatre, a winning smile and the ability to deliver the most spectacular cocktail ever are just the beginning. The ability to also converse with a perfect stranger, be a therapist and have your game on at 3am takes it to the next level.

Perhaps, like me, you marvel at their ability to memorise ingredients and ratios to produce the perfect cocktail in a matter of moments. Designing new cocktail creations may seem well out of reach, and through being spoilt for choice with the seemingly endless array of spirits, mixers and finishes, you may find it hard to know where to begin.

The best approach to making your own impressive drinks is to start with some of the simpler cocktail classics and the more basic techniques. Master those and you'll be inspired to build your repertoire. This chapter covers the techniques, while the drinks and cocktails can be found in the chapters in part IV.

mastering the basic techniques

Practising some of the basic bartending techniques – and knowing when to use them – will help you to learn and appreciate different flavour combinations and to understand how they best perform with other ingredients. You'll soon discover your personal preferences when it comes to cocktail styles and, before you know it, you'll be creating your own.

shake

Shake your ingredients when the recipe calls for blending juices, syrups, dairy and (non-carbonated) mixers. This emulsifies and aerates the ingredients and ensures you have a well-blended liquid.

Shaking changes the overall texture of the ingredients, minimises splitting of ingredients and will generally give the cocktail a cloudy appearance.

Use a cobbler or Boston shaker – see the next chapter for more on these options.

Add all ingredients first then lots of ice. Where possible, use larger blocks of ice to avoid chipping the ice and diluting the cocktail. Make sure you seal the two cups or parts of the shaker well (no-one wants to clean a cocktail off the walls), and hold firmly together with both hands when shaking. To ensure the ingredients blend well, shake for 10 to 15 seconds.

The ice not only chills the drink, but a small amount of the melted water will also transfer into the drink.

dry-shake

Dry-shaking refers to the mixing of ingredients without ice. Any cocktail that includes egg whites or cream benefits from a vigorous dry-shake to not only emulsify the ingredients but also aerate them, in order to produce a thicker foam on the finished cocktail.

After a dry-shake, add ice and shake again to cool down the cocktail mix.

Some mixologists prefer to reverse dry-shake. This entails shaking all the ingredients together first with ice, and then straining the cocktail mix and shaking again without the ice. In other words, chill first and then aerate.

stir

Stirring is called for when you have a number of spirit ingredients that don't so much require vigorous emulsifying but a gentler blend. When the act of shaking is a more intense method of blending, the stirring takes a little longer, avoids ice shards breaking off and diluting the mix and delivers a cool (not over-chilled), clear-spirited drink.

The general law of mixology is if using clear, alcohol-only ingredients, stir. The stirring time is usually around 30 to 50 seconds.

throw

Throwing (also known as rolling) is fun, but takes a little practice. This technique involves pouring ingredients from one shaker to another and is most commonly used when you don't want to over-agitate the ingredients. This is also where the theatre of mixology comes into play.

You need a Boston shaker and Hawthorne strainer (see the next chapter). Fill one part of the shaker with ice and seal with the strainer, and fill the other half with the ingredients. Pour ingredients from one half to the other and back again five or six times. As you master the technique, 'draw' out the pour by pulling the strainer side away from the receiving cup as you pour. Throwing is used when making cocktails such as a Bloody Mary or Red Snapper – so needs to be practised well to avoid the look of tomato 'blood' on the walls.

build

Building a cocktail refers to the adding of ingredients one by one straight into the glass. Add a swizzle stick for stirring (and fiddling!).

blend

Blending is not so much a skill set that requires mastering, but a technique that bars use for making certain cocktails.

Most often used to make frozen cocktails (by adding crushed ice) or for heavier ingredients (such as solid fruits or ice cream), adding blended cocktails will certainly increase your cocktail offering.

muddle

To be clear, muddling is not mashing. The function of muddling is to gently break down the ingredients in order to extract their flavour or juices into your drink. You're not trying to pulp the ingredients to within an inch of their life, but crush them gently to release their essence and aroma.

Muddling is best done in a steel shaker. If using a glass receptacle, make sure the glass is thick with a solid base and designed to take the pressure of the muddling.

If you don't have a muddler, an alternative is to use a mortar and pestle, tamper, wooden spoon or the end of a wooden rolling pin. If using a wooden implement, make sure it isn't lacquered because you don't want any paint or lacquer ending up in your drink. To feel like a pro and master the technique, invest in a muddler to make it easy and enjoyable. They're well worth the small investment.

The technique required to muddle is to repeatedly push down on the ingredients and twist. Repeat numerous times in order to extract the flavour.

strain

Straining is an integral step in the process for most cocktails. After the vigorous activity of shaking and/or muddling your cocktail ingredients, the straining process removes any unwanted fragments, such as small fruit particles, damaged leaves or herbs or fine ice shards. It also prevents your shaker ice from falling into your cocktail glass.

A more recent bar habit is to 'double-strain' or 'fine-strain' the drink. This involves pouring the liquid into your glass via a second hand-held strainer. In other words, you double-strain your cocktail from shaker to glass in one pour.

In the case where your ingredients have finer particles that you want to ensure don't make it to the glass, you may consider double-straining. Whether this is entirely necessary is up to you. Aside from the washing up of a fine strainer (which doesn't sit high on the list of tasks I love and tends to take away from a wonderful cocktail experience), a proper-functioning Hawthorne or julep strainer should do the job.

squeeze

A recipe may call for squeezing a slice of citrus peel over your drink. Hold the peel facing away from you and towards the glass to release a small amount of the oils from the peel and imbue the drink with a beautiful aroma.

spank

Sounds kinky, but this is simply the technique of bringing out the best in your leafy garnish.

When your cocktail calls for a green garnish – such as mint, basil, thyme or rosemary – place it in the palm of your hand and quickly spank it with your other palm. The motion is like a clap, with the garnish between the two palms.

This releases the oils in the leaf, keeps it looking fresh and new and creates a good first (and fragrant) impression for your cocktail.

sweeten

Most cocktails that call for a little sweetener make reference to a 'simple syrup'. This is a basic sugar syrup that you can easily make yourself at home. All you need is equal parts (1:1) sugar and water, which are boiled in a small saucepan until the sugar has dissolved and the mixture resembles a viscous syrup. Take the syrup off the heat (don't let it turn into toffee!) and allow to cool. Then pour the syrup into a sterilised glass bottle to be stored in the fridge.

If you want to make flavoured syrups, add your preferred ingredient, such as fruit, spice or herbs, once the sugar has dissolved and the syrup is about ready to thicken. Remove the syrup from the heat and let the flavours infuse for about 30 minutes while cooling down. Once cooled, strain into your bottle for storing.

Now that you have an understanding of the techniques, the next step is to discover the essential tools you need to create some of your favourite cocktails.

CHAPTER 11

home bar essentials

(and a few non-essentials…)

Of all the gin joints in all the towns in all the world, she walks into mine.

RICK BLAINE (HUMPHREY BOGART'S CHARACTER IN *CASABLANCA*)

When it comes to stocking up your home bar, it's easy to go a little wild, and the list of what could be included is extensive. And regardless of how serious you might like this bar of yours to be, you no doubt want it to reflect your own style, taste and drinking palate. Going all in and buying up everything you can get your hands on might be fun for a day, but having a budget in mind is also wise.

Apart from stocking a range of commonly used liquors and mixers, you will also need some essential bar and cocktail accessories that not only look good, but also enhance your cocktail-making skills and experience in the same way a decent set of knives improves your skills in the kitchen. The right tools will also produce better looking – and, of course, tasting – cocktails.

The best approach is to start with a few of the essentials and build from there. Having a 'little bit of everything' or stocking what you won't typically use or even need just doesn't make sense. Instead, customise your bar around what you actually drink and what you'd like to play around with.

In this chapter is a list of the top bar accessories to help you produce some impressive cocktail creations. To help you plan your purchases, I've split the list into two:

- the needs
- the wants.

the needs ...

Everything included here will make your cocktails shine. While quite a few items are listed, most are easy to find, affordable and (hopefully) won't need replacing too often.

bar spoons

Bar spoons have become an art form in themselves, with some beautifully designed options that would make anyone feel like a professional mixologist by simply owning one.

Putting this aside, they need to be functional, and the function of a bar spoon is to stir. Choose one with a long twisted handle to make it easy to grip and stir. The standard length of a bar spoon is around 30 centimetres, allowing you to manoeuvre the spoon efficiently in a tall glass, as well as keeping your sleeves nice and dry.

Bar spoons allow you to gently stir the ingredients without breaking down the ice. They also assist in building layered drinks by pouring a second liquid down the back of the spoon or handle to create a visually appealing layered or 'stacked' effect.

bottle opener and corkscrew

Every bar needs a bottle opener. And, while the days of the cork feel numbered, a corkscrew still needs to hold pride of place in the bar for that bottle that insists on keeping the tradition of the cork alive.

glassware

When it comes to glassware, the offerings are almost limitless, as are the price points. Some stunning glasses are available, but you only need a few to get started – depending, of course, on the drink and the occasion.

Believe it or not, the glassware can make a difference to how your drink will look and taste. Everything from the shape of the rim, the weight of the glass, the space inside, and the shape and feel of the glass in your hand do enhance your drinking experience.

rocks/double old-fashioned

The rocks glass is used for serving straight spirits or mixed drinks over ice balls or cubes. They're squat, with a wide opening and thick base, but sophisticated.

The rocks glass is ideal for drinks you build in the glass and/or require muddling.

collins/highball

You only need either a Collins or a highball option, unless you're a high-end expert (and, if this is the case, you probably don't need this list). A Collins glass is usually slightly taller and narrower than a highball, with a touch more capacity.

Both options are tall and cylindrical, and typically used for cold drinks requiring lots of ice and larger ratios of non-alcoholic mixers.

coupe glass

The coupe glass is an elegant bowl-shaped glass on a long stem, originally designed for champagne. It's ideal for the cocktail normally prepared in a shaker and served in the glass without ice. They're also popular for the martini because they're easier to handle and hold a little more than a martini glass.

martini glass

Despite the coupe glass being a more than satisfactory substitute, if you're a martini fiend and relish a 'James Bond' moment, then the martini glass it is. Perhaps the most iconic and best-recognised cocktail glass of them all, the martini glass's conical shape is designed to open up the liquid, enhancing the drink's flavours and aromas. The long stem keeps your hands away from the body of the glass to prevent warming up the liquid.

cocktail shaker

Here's where it gets real.

The cocktail shaker is your greatest friend. Always go for metal (as opposed to glass), because it's better at keeping cocktails cool – and is harder to break, so you avoid the whole experience ending in tears with breakage. Any dints you may accumulate from enthusiastic cocktail shaking simply add character to the metal cup.

A shaker is essential for cocktail making when the recipe calls for a shaker to be used (obvious, I know, but people have been known to improvise). Shaking ensures proper blending of ingredients of varying viscosities, particularly when using spirits, juices, egg or dairy. A shaker also performs the function of aerating your cocktail to give you a light and frothy, blended finish.

When a cocktail calls for a shaker, you have three types to choose from:

1. the cobbler (the traditional style)
2. the Boston (the preferred style)
3. the French/Parisian (the classy French one).

the cobbler shaker

The cobbler tends to be the household favourite. It's stylish in design, easy to use and a one-stop shop when it comes to cocktail making for the novice. With an in-built strainer and measuring lid to replace the need for a jigger, the cobbler is certainly an attractive and versatile option for your home bar.

the boston shaker

The Boston is the preferred choice for bartenders and wannabe cocktail pros. This version has two shakers – either one metal and one glass shaker or two metal shakers. In the case of two metal shakers, the larger tin is called the 'Boston' (28 oz) and the smaller tin is called the 'Toby' (18 oz).

While the Boston style doesn't include an in-built strainer or measure, it does make for easier cleaning and is quicker to use (and re-use, particularly if you're punching out the cocktails at a rate). However, some skill is required to ensure the two cups are securely sealed before shaking your cocktail onto your shirt instead of into your glass.

If choosing the Boston shaker, lean towards a bottom weighted tin.

the french/parisian shaker

This sleek number is a classy design combo of the Boston and the cobbler – it has two shakers like the Boston, but looks more like the cobbler. Beautiful to look at and easy to use, the French/Parisian shaker is a centuries-old style that has undoubtedly stood the test of time.

cocktail strainer

A cocktail made well should not only look good, but also taste delicious. Cocktail strainers play an important role in achieving this by separating the non-essentials in your cocktail mix from the lovely elixir that becomes your cocktail drink.

You have three types of cocktail strainers to choose from:

1. Hawthorne strainer
2. fine mesh strainer
3. julep strainer.

Of these, the essentials I recommend are the Hawthorne and fine mesh strainer.

hawthorne strainer

This is an absolute must, particularly if you decide to head down the Boston shaker path.

Modelled on the traditional Chinese tea strainers, the Hawthorne found the limelight when fresh, clean ice became available all year round, and straining drinks evolved from optional to essential.

Surprisingly, the name 'Hawthorne' didn't originate from the surname of its inventor (whose name, by the way, was William Wright), but was actually named after an erstwhile bar in Boston called the Hawthorne Café.

The Hawthorne strainer consists of a flat stainless steel disk at the end of a handle, with a removable wire spring attached around the edge of the metal disk.

The strainer fits neatly inside the lip of the Boston shaker and is designed to allow fine fruit pulp to pass through, while keeping ice and unwanted chunks from ending up in your glass.

mesh strainer

While the Hawthorne strainer separates your cocktail from unwanted larger pieces, the mesh strainer removes the finer pulp, shards of ice and other small solids, such as seeds, from your cocktail.

The finer mesh strainer is typically held over the glass and directly beneath the Hawthorne strainer when pouring your cocktail from the shaker to your glass, enabling you to double strain the cocktail.

Double straining is well worth the effort in order to achieve thorough filtration of your cocktail. Both strainers are inexpensive and well worth the spend if you're looking for a smooth and silky cocktail finish.

julep strainer

Although not essential, the julep strainer is worthy of an honourable mention, if for no other reason than to highlight its somewhat fascinating history, as well as acknowledging its status as the first strainer officially used for cocktails.

The julep first hit the market in the mid-1800s and was designed to be used for drinking Mint Julep cocktails, with the strainer sitting inside the glass. Its slightly curved, slotted spoon design enabled cocktail enthusiasts to enjoy a tipple without the ice falling onto their face when they tilted the glass, which is why it was originally referred to as an 'ice spoon'.

The primary function of the julep strainer is best compared to drinking straws used today. Not as elegant to use but certainly more sustainable.

pourers

Cheap as chips and the one accessory that genuinely makes you feel like a professional, bottle pourers replace the lid on your bottle. While they don't pour a specific, measured amount, they do help with consistency.

The pourer also minimises dripping and over-pouring, enabling you to work efficiently when building your cocktails.

jiggers

The 'jigger' is the official name for the gadget that ensures a correct, measured pour every time. Jiggers come in different sizes, ranging from 15 ml to 75 ml, and are essential for your home bar to ensure the cocktail ingredients are correctly measured, helping you deliver a consistently delicious cocktail every time.

Jiggers can come double-ended, with the larger end a standard jigger size and the smaller end known as a 'pony shot'.

muddler

The cocktail muddler is like the pestle for your drinks. Used correctly, it adds dimension to your cocktail by releasing the flavour and aroma from your ingredients to infuse your drink.

A good muddler should have a long handle to avoid hitting your hand on the side of the glass or cocktail shaker, and ergonomically designed for easy holding.

Choose a muddler that is unpainted and unvarnished, to avoid any flecks eventually coming off in your drinks after prolonged use.

mixing glass

A mixing glass is not unlike a glass jug. Its function as a vessel is to mix your cocktails, as opposed to the shaker where your cocktails need a more prolonged, vigorous mix. The key is to ensure the glass is thick enough to allow for a bar spoon or muddler to bang around and not risk breaking or chipping the glass.

The mixing glass must have a pourer or spout (you don't want to lose a drop when pouring) and, ideally, be at least 750 ml in size.

ice kit

Ice – and its size – plays a significant role in cocktail making. If your ice cubes are too small, your drink is susceptible to ice diluting your drink; too large, and you have nowhere left in the glass to fit the cocktail. For mixing cocktails, look for an ice tray with roughly 3 cm squares. For serving a spirit or mixed drink over ice, look out for the 5 cm ball moulds. The spheres melt slower, keep your drink chilled and make for a highly pleasant and sophisticated drinking experience.

cutting board and (sharp!) knife

A good sharp knife and a non-slip cutting board are useful for slicing up various garnishes for your cocktails. The cutting board also provides a hygienic, dedicated space when working with fresh cocktail ingredients.

juicer

A citrus juicer is a mainstay for your bar. While pre-packaged juices are available when you can't find the time to squeeze yourself, nothing replaces the flavour of using freshly squeezed lemon, orange, lime or grapefruit in your drink.

The basic handheld juicer is sufficient for most needs. Alternatively, a number of showpiece items are available that increase juicing efficiency, particularly if you're making a lot of juice-based cocktails.

tools for those finishing touches

Many great cocktails are only complete once the finishing touches are added – and some specific tools are useful in making those last touches so much easier.

peeler

Citrus peel is a perfect finish that most cocktails cannot do without. To ensure your garnish is all peel and no bitter white pith, source a quality, stainless steel peeler sharp enough to cleanly remove just the peel.

zester

A zester is a useful tool that enables you to remove the citrus zest from the fruit. Unlike a grater, the zester has smaller holes that shave a much finer zest from the skin. Although it's not used as frequently in the bar as a peeler, the zester is handy to have when you need a dusting of fine, citrus curls (such as lemon or lime) on top of your cocktail. It also works well to avoid collecting the pith when peeling or shaving the citrus peel.

microplane

Another decorative garnish option, and a very useful tool alongside the zester, is a microplane grater. The microplane is easy to work with over your cocktail glass and delivers a fluffier citrus powder, rather than zesty curls. If you're a fan of the margarita, you'll enjoy using this.

tweezers

Put aside the fact that tweezers are just a practical tool for delicately picking up and garnishing your cocktails – they also add an element of flair and theatre when adding the final touches with precision.

Also known as cocktail garnish tongs, tweezers are particularly handy to have when you're adding a garnish inside a highball – so look for a pair around 25 to 30 cm long. It makes for a much more pleasant drinking experience if your fingers haven't been fishing around in your drink before serving.

the wants ...

And now we get to the 'nice to haves'. Although not completely necessary, they do add to the overall experience (and you do look good having them!).

bar mat

Even if not essential, bar mats are still incredibly useful (and not terribly expensive). Bar mats are handy for working on when preparing your drinks. They catch spills and protect the bar's surface from wet glasses and moisture.

ice bucket

If you're keen to deck out your home bar with some of the less-essential, but nevertheless useful, items, there's always room for a good-looking ice bucket.

The added benefit is that it can double as a wine bucket or chiller for pre-mixed cocktails.

ice crusher

A number of cocktails call for crushed ice. Although more likely found in a commercial cocktail bar, having an ice crusher on hand certainly extends the home-made cocktail repertoire.

Numerous options are on the market. If you decide you really 'need' one, consider a portable option that doesn't take up too much space behind the bar.

glass rack

If you're fortunate to have a dedicated space for a proper home bar, glass racks are a useful way to store your stem glasses safely. They help to minimise breakages when stored in cupboards or on the bench, while also allowing for easy access when making cocktails.

Racks also provide for efficient storage, particularly when wall-mounted or installed overhead.

cocktail rimmer

I was a little torn as to whether this should be a want or a need. For the sake of balance and budget, the cocktail rimmer found its way into the 'wants', but it's a seriously cool cocktail gadget to have.

Enough to turn you to drink just to have an excuse of owning one, a cocktail rimmer makes it easy for you to add a sugar or salt rim on your glass as a recipe requires to enhance the cocktail's flavour.

If you're making margaritas, martinis, mojitos, or any other cocktail that benefits from a sweet or salty rim, a cocktail rimmer will become a necessary bar essential before you know it.

If you do decide to make the purchase, choose one with three tiers – one section for sugar, one for salt and one for the liquid sponge that makes the ingredients stick to the glass.

dehydrator

With a bit of research (and an oven), you can easily make your own dehydrated fruit garnishes without the need of a standalone dehydrator. However, this section is all about the 'wants', and dehydrators are a cocktail maker's best friend and a great tool to have, allowing you to safely 'set-and-forget' when dehydrating.

These come in varying sizes, styles and prices, so do your homework.

don't forget the liquids …

It's one thing to have the tools of the trade. Now you need the liquids.

Some of the liquid essentials to include on your list include:

- bourbon
- citrus juices and garnishes
- gins (of course)
- liqueurs
- rum
- sodas and mixers
- vodka
- whisky

With the exception of your gins and mixers (yes, I am biased), most of these ingredients don't need to be top-shelf in quality or price, particularly when your cocktails are modelled around the gin being your hero ingredient.

... or the ice

Ice is one of the most important essentials in a bartender's kit. If you can afford to be a little choosy, find ice cube trays that produce larger than normal cubes.

As mentioned, ice balls are fantastic for serving a straight spirit or mixed drink over ice. Silicon moulds are readily available for these and the outcome is well worth the small effort to find them. The benefit of larger ice pieces is that they melt more slowly, keep your drink super-chilled and look fabulous.

Wherever possible, use filtered water to make your ice. You are less likely to contaminate your drink or have any unpleasant residue in your drink with clean, freshly filtered water.

Of course, as you try new cocktails, you'll find the list of required tools and ingredients will grow. Start with the basics, follow the cocktails that appeal to you and go (and grow) from there.

Once you start, I'm sure you'll struggle to stop.

PART IV

MIXING DRINKS

CHAPTER 12

the classic g&t

Gin and tonic have saved more Englishmen's lives and minds than all the doctors in the Empire.

SIR WINSTON CHURCHILL

It seems deserving that the opening chapter in this part be dedicated to one of the world's best loved – and most consumed – cocktails ... the gin & tonic.

the birth of a classic ...

The birth of the classic G&T, quite by chance it may seem, evolved from necessity and survival.

I'm sure we can all relate.

As the history books tell us, one consequence (among many others) of the British Crown taking over the governance of India was British immigrants falling to the plight of malaria. These immigrants, along with English sailors travelling to India (and other destinations where malaria was rife), relied on quinine rations to help prevent and fight the life-threatening disease.

Quinine was a local remedy delivered from the bark of the South American cinchona tree (also known as the 'fever tree', because of its ability to stop chills). The use of the bark was first introduced to Europe sometime in the 1640s, where it was believed to be a preventative and cure-all against malaria.

It is likely that quinine, in a crystal form, was shipped as quinine tablets or grains to the various colonial outposts for their own medicinal use. One would simply drop a single grain into a bottle of soda water to make their own tonic. While quinine was considered a type of miracle cure, it was notoriously hideous and bitter in taste. To make it more palatable, the quinine powder and soda was mixed with a good dose of sugar. As a consequence, tonic water was created.

Quinine remained an important medicinal remedy through to the 20th century and even for treating soldiers in the Pacific during World War II – so much so that the last American plane to fly out of the Philippines before the area was taken over by the Japanese carried over 4 million quinine seeds.

As the drink evolved, gin was added, largely because it was thought to aid digestion. Next, lime was added to also help offset the bitterness of the quinine. However – seeing so many sailors were now drinking the gin and tonic – the lime's primary function was to help prevent scurvy, a common disease found in sailors and pirates due to their long periods at sea, which meant very limited access to fresh fruit and vegetables. The high vitamin C content found in the lime, and its ability to withstand long journeys, was an essential daily dose in the seaman's diet.

Now the traditional G&T was complete with its four ingredients – gin, tonic, ice and lime. Because gin travelled on rocking ships significantly better than beer, the combination of gin and tonic water made for a way to unwind, keep healthy and, with a squeeze of lime for vitamin C to prevent scurvy, you have the classic – and perhaps the world's best known – gin cocktail that today continues to be an all-round favourite.

who ultimately 'invented' tonic water?

We can thank the British for coming up with the idea to mix quinine, soda water and sugar together, and for the idea of adding a squeeze of lime to the mix. As to who was the first to commercially produce tonic water, we can accredit this to a gentleman named Erasmus Bond, owner of Pitt & Co, who was awarded the first patent for tonic water in 1858. Pitt's aerated tonic water was promoted as a digestive tonic, designed to strengthen the digestive organs and tone the whole nervous system, promote appetite and restore a stomach that had been weakened by an excess of indulgence.

Another businessman named Johann Jacob (JJ) Schweppe, fascinated with the process of carbonating beverages, founded the Schweppes company in Geneva in 1783. But it wasn't until sometime later that his company, seeing the interest and apparent need for a quinine-flavoured water, came up with its own quinine and lime-infused mineral water. This product was released in 1870 and soon penetrated the market. Unfortunately, Mr Schweppe died in 1821, so did not live to see this day, nor appreciate the success of his company's Indian Tonic Water.

quinine's value today

When the healing properties of the Peruvian cinchona bark were first discovered around 1630, it was initially used to treat a fever. Until it was replaced by synthetic anti-malarial remedies in around the 1940s, cinchona (and quinine) was the only known effective treatment in the West.

Nowadays, in order to be effective, the required quinine intake for treating malaria is significantly higher than what is permitted in commercially produced tonic water (less than 85 mg per litre). Furthermore, resistance to quinine has been increasing since the 1980s.

So to be clear, relying on G&Ts to get you through a bout of malaria would not be wise. Despite this revelation, folklore still exists that a G&T (or few) will keep the mozzies away on a hot summer's night.

how to make a bloody good g&t

Gone are the days where the only G&T found was in Nanna's glass and (heaven forbid) not our own. Trends come and go, but the G&T has evolved dramatically since the 1990s and what was once old is now new again. Never before have more time, energy and effort been dedicated to mastering this incredible drink.

Despite being one of the simplest cocktails to make, the G&T also seems to be the most heavily contested, and certainly requires a few variables to be on point. Your favourite glass, the ideal gin, well-prepared ice (how much, how big, what shape?), the perfectly paired tonic and the right garnish to complement your preferred gin-of-the-moment all need to be considered. And remembering that the perfect G&T is all about your own personal taste is also important.

To keep it simple and avoid sweating on the small stuff, the ideal and recommended ratio of gin to tonic is somewhere between 1:1 and 1:3. After all, you want the gin to shine through (it's not called a gin and tonic for nothing), but also appreciate the presence of a damn good tonic.

Keep in mind, the ratio of gin to tonic largely depends on your personal taste and preference. The alcohol by volume (ABV) of a gin also plays a role in how much tonic to add.

Finding your perfect G&T is all about what you enjoy. So let's begin. Four ingredients are key – gin, tonic, ice and garnish. But before you delve into these key elements, you need to consider what to put it in …

the glass

We've all had those days where a bucket will suffice, and we've all had those days when it's the only vessel big enough to cater for your shitty end-of-the-day download. However, if you want to keep it a little classy, go conventional with a highball, or choose a balloon-style glass to allow the botanicals some space to open up a little.

If the opportunity is there (in other words, you planned for this), use a glass that is chilled.

the gin

We are well and truly spoilt for choice when it comes to choosing gin. Some gins seem to have been tailored to deliver the perfect G&T, while others are a little too tricky – and best used in other cocktails or with alternate mixers.

The gin is the star in your G&T show so, wherever possible, choose a good-quality gin. Remember, though, that stars rarely succeed on their own and good support is needed, which is where your garnish, tonic and ice come into play.

Once upon a time, I would have suggested a classic London Dry gin as your ideal choice. However, some exceptional contemporary, flavoured gins will also deliver an awesome G&T experience.

One of the best gins to use for a G&T is a navy strength gin. Because the higher alcohol strength holds more of the essential oils and flavours from a gin's botanicals, the gin carries an extra kick of flavour, not always experienced in a lower proof gin. When adding tonic water to your gin, the higher proof gin tends to stand up to the tonic better, making it difficult for the tonic water to overpower the botanicals and flavours of the gin. After all, you want to enjoy both the gin and the tonic, not just one or the other.

the tonic

Never underestimate the power of the tonic. Again, personal taste and preference is paramount, but when you consider that the tonic comprises the majority of the drink, you start to realise why you should choose wisely.

A good marriage between tonic and gin is one where they each complement the other. You should be able to taste your gin (which is why we don't go over the top with the tonic), and appreciate the value that tonic water brings to your glass.

As my good friends at CAPI say, 'The role of the tonic is to be the bridesmaid to the gin bride.' As a gin producer, I couldn't have said it better myself.

A vast range of premium tonic waters are now available in the market place, so choosing the right one can be as challenging as finding your favourite gin. At this point, it's worth keeping in mind that you're not trying to find the solution to world peace, so avoid getting too stressed about which tonic water is the best and remember that your palate will tell you what you enjoy.

for the non-tonic lovers ...

The main reasons people have an aversion to the G&T are usually the substandard tonics used, the lack of chill in the glass and/or the wrong ratios of tonic to gin. So if you don't favour (or perhaps even despise) G&Ts, it may simply be a case of not having yet discovered a tonic you enjoy.

While tonic water is typically and traditionally bitter in taste, we are now spoilt for choice, particularly with the extensive range of artisan brands and flavours available to choose from. The emphasis on using real quinine, rather than artificial flavouring, has also dramatically improved the overall tonic experience.

Having said that, the power of the tonic is not to be underestimated, and the right mixer can make the gin. The fun is in the ongoing journey to discover your own version of G&T excellence.

Sweeter tonics, for example, can be a little overpowering for some, but you may find they open the G&T door for you across to the brighter side of gin.

And don't forget that the stocky-standard 'pub' G&T is too often made using the cheapest of gins with an overload of even cheaper tonic. Sometimes the ratio may be as high as 1:9 or 1:10. To be clear, that is not what a gin purist would call a G&T.

But if tonic water really isn't your thing, substitute it for soda water or lemonade. As mentioned in chapter 8, another increasingly popular alternative is to go for the 'sonic' – a mix of tonic and soda water. This mix tones down the bitter tonic flavour, but keeps the flavour of the G&T alive, just with a little less intensity.

the ice

Let's be honest – when it hits gin o'clock, any ice will do. However, any ice won't necessarily deliver the perfect tipple, so taking some time to prepare the best ice you can is well worth the effort.

Use ice that is absolutely, completely frozen and has been made with clean, quality water (filtered water is good). Poor-tasting water has the ability to contaminate your drink.

Perhaps counterintuitively, using more ice actually leads to less dilution, so filling the glass to the top with ice is essential. This will slow down the melting process, which minimises the diluting of your G&T. Using a chilled glass helps slow down the ice melt further.

the garnish

Traditionally, the garnish of choice is a wedge or slice of lime or lemon. Either option is usually a safe and delicious choice, adding a bit of spunk to your gin.

However, with such diversity in the vast array of gins to choose from, it would be wrong to assume that either/or will work with any gin. Limes tend to have a brighter, bolder flavour whereas lemons deliver a more subtle, delicate outcome and tend to pair well with a gin's botanicals.

One reliable rule is to choose a garnish that will complement one or more of the botanicals that feature in your gin. Consider what flavours you're looking to accentuate from the gin you've chosen. For example, if orange is a botanical used, try using an orange garnish. If you'd like to draw out the peppery notes, add a few peppercorns.

Avoiding getting too heavy-handed in your use of garnish. You don't need to squeeze the citrus garnish all through your drink, particularly if you're using a quality gin.

Remember that all the elements should come together to bring you a very pleasant – and memorable – drinking experience. You don't want to taste the garnish, or the tonic, or just the gin or strange-tasting ice. You want to enjoy a well-blended, unforgettable G&T.

What you should also remember is that, like your choice of tonic, the garnish you choose should not be used to camouflage a poor-quality gin.

By now, you've probably generated a real thirst for a drink, so let's bring these elements together and make that bloody good G&T.

A bloody good g&t

Ingredients and equipment:

50 ml quality gin

100 ml (or 150 ml if you must) good-quality tonic water; if using a navy strength gin, you may need to add 150–250 ml.

Wedge of lemon or lime (or your choice of garnish)

Highball or balloon-style glass

Ice (lots)

Method:

1. Fill a chilled glass to the top with ice cubes.
2. Add 50 ml of gin.
3. Top up with tonic water.
4. Garnish with your preferred garnish.
5. Gently 'lift' the liquid with a long slim spoon or stirrer, doing your best to avoid losing any fizz.
6. Waste no more time, your job is done.

CHAPTER 13

the gin martini

> One martini is all right. Two are too many,
> and three are not enough.
>
> JAMES THURBER

The Holy Grail of cocktails – certainly the most controversial and arguably the hardest to make – the martini has captivated generations. This cocktail is one that establishes class and status, and defines sophistication and understated elegance. It's the cocktail most likely responsible for debauched nights we'd rather forget, but also the drink we choose to impress and perfect. It's effortless, elegant, sophisticated and timeless. It has a glass dedicated to it, its own garnish and is even endorsed by a fictional British Secret Service agent.

One thing is certain: the martini has a history (both famous and infamous) well worthy of a chapter dedicated to it.

Despite its minimal ingredient list, the definition of the 'perfect' martini remains in contention. Ratios are (almost) everything, but also important are the selection of ingredients and garnish – and, of course, whether it's shaken or stirred.

I read somewhere that if you're lonely, make a martini – because someone will soon be over your shoulder telling you how you're doing it wrong, with another person contradicting them. We all need a first-world problem, so mastering the ideal martini might as well be that problem.

At the end of the day, the perfect martini is probably best described as the one that you enjoy the most.

It would also be fair to say that the perfect martini relies on finding the perfect balance and harmony using only a handful of elements. But when you are spoilt for choice in which of those elements to choose, creating such harmony is almost on par with man's search for meaning (a universal dilemma).

the martini's history

Validating the history of the martini is almost a more arduous task than perfecting one – because, like all great stories shared after a few, the origin of the martini is often in dispute.

One theory is that the name was derived from the Martini & Rossi brand of vermouth, which was first created in the mid-1800s. (The company name was changed to Martini & Rossi in 1879.)

Another suggestion is that the martini evolved from the Martinez, a cocktail that was first created in the 1860s at the Occidental Hotel in San Francisco. It was said to be the drink of choice for people taking the evening ferry from San Francisco to a town called Martinez, also in California. Residents of Martinez insist that the cocktail was first created by a bartender in their town, while other sources suggest the cocktail was named after the town itself.

Perhaps the most famous (and quite possibly legendary) story around the birth of the martini takes this connection between the drink and the town of Martinez, and adds some more specifics. This story centres on the legendary US barman Jerry Thomas. Thomas wrote the first ever cocktail book, *Bartender's Guide*, first published in 1862.

In Thomas's story, a tired, dusty traveller stops through a bar Thomas was keeping at the time in San Francisco. The traveller wanted something new to drink. Thomas asked the man where he was heading and the traveller said Martinez. In that moment, Thomas is said to have prepared the very first Martinez, mixing gin, vermouth and bitters. Over time, while the ingredients continued to be experimented with, the name was abbreviated to martini. The first published recipe for a martini was in Harry Johnson's Bartender's Manual produced in 1888, listing its ingredients as Old Tom gin, sweet vermouth, orange curacao, gomme (the French word for gum) syrup, bitters and a lemon twist.

While the martini is largely considered an American creation, by the 20th century it was also widely popular in Europe. The British Prime Minister, Winston Churchill, was a massive fan. However, when shipments of vermouth from Italy or France became scarce during World War II, Churchill's interpretation of a martini was to combine 'ice-cold gin and a bow in the direction of France'.

Even without a war on, the ingredients and ratios in a martini have always been up to personal interpretation. Alfred Hitchcock's preferred martini recipe, for example, was 'five parts gin and a quick glance at a bottle of vermouth', while Clark Gable simply ran a vermouth cork around the rim of the glass.

Despite the somewhat ambiguous theories on the martini's origins and the many variations on what to include, the key is mastering this ever-popular cocktail to suit your taste. Without adding too much pressure, you have dozens of variations and recipes to choose from. With the added pressure of countless gins also available, the best approach is to narrow down the essentials and go from there.

But one important question first ...

shaken or stirred?

Heated debate tends to circle around whether a martini should be shaken or stirred. In one sense, Harry Johnson's 1900 edition of the *Bartender's Manual* put to bed such controversy by including two martini recipes. One was for a Martini Cocktail and the other was for a Bradford a la Martini. The crucial difference between the two was that the Martini

Cocktail was to be stirred, and the Bradford shaken. Adopting this principle, any martini shaken therefore becomes a Bradford.

The *Stork Club Bar Book*, first published in 1946, states that the only 'real difference is the appearance', and further suggests that bartenders should 'prefer to stir but certainly oblige a customer if they wished shaken'.

And as for the iconic 007, in the first Bond novel from 1953, Casino Royale (and in its 2006 film adaptation), James was actually the 'shaken not stirred' Vesper Martini man, favouring his martini with gin, vodka and Kina Lillet vermouth with a twist of lemon. As noted, the martini is usually stirred instead of shaken, so Bond's style was already subversive. In later novels, Bond orders regular vodka martinis, and regular gin martinis, but by the time the novels became films, Bond's liking of vodka martinis, shaken not stirred, was fully established.

Fun fact: When the film version of James Bond headed down the vodka martini path in the 1960s, an entire generation decided to follow suit. Unfortunately, this coincided with the growing trend towards drinking vodka and the movement away from gin in the United States, a troubling fact for gin producers. Fortunately, the famous blue bottle – Bombay Sapphire, launched in 1986 – slowly but surely penetrated its way into the vodka-loving market, and is deemed to have played a pivotal role in the gin resurgence that we are still enjoying today.

When considering your preference for 'shaken' or 'stirred', keep in mind that ordering a shaken martini tends to deliver a more diluted drink. The vigorous activity of shaking breaks off small pieces of ice that quickly melt and dilute the cocktail's ingredients. Shaking also adds air to your drink, whereas stirring will blend the ingredients together while keeping them smooth and less agitated.

other serving alternatives ...

If shaken or stirred don't rock your martini boat, here are a few alternatives:

- **Straight up:** Your martini is prepared on ice but strained straight into your glass – sans shake or stir.

- **Thrown:** Not so commonly seen or done but certainly delivers a great martini. This requires the maker to pour a martini from the shaker held up high directly into a shaker held low. Visually impressive, and somewhat challenging for the novice, this technique functionally provides the added benefit of releasing the aromatics of the vermouth and gin, and delivers a super smooth martini.

- **With a twist:** This refers to the choice of citrus peel that is gently twisted into your glass and usually ends up as a spiral garnish in your martini. The twist of the citrus releases oils into your cocktail. Choosing the right citrus is crucial and can make or break the character of your gin and martini experience.

basic martini making rules

In theory, you could be mistaken for thinking a martini is one of the easiest cocktails to make. At first glance, this should be the case, particularly when there are essentially only a handful of ingredients, starting with gin and vermouth.

However, a truly memorable martini deserves a high standard of care and attention. It relies on pairing your key ingredients well, along with an attention to detail in the preparation and a level of commitment that reflects your desire to deliver a martini that matters.

Whether you're a purist or tend to take a more relaxed approach to making cocktails, here are some basic rules for making a great martini:

- Ingredients:
  - For a classic martini, use a London Dry gin.
  - The more dry vermouth you use, the 'wetter' the martini is.
  - The less dry vermouth used, the 'drier' the martini.
  - Choosing a gin you enjoy is important because the flavour profile and character of your gin will be the feature in your martini. Budget ingredients have no place here.

- Glassware:
    - Where possible, always use a martini glass.
    - Chill your glass by placing it in the fridge or freezer before making your drink.
    - Shake or stir. If your martini contains only spirits (such as gin and vermouth), gently stir the ingredients in a glass or shaker with ice for about a minute. If you're heading down the path of a martini with fruit juices, add all ingredients into a cocktail shaker and shake for 8 to 10 seconds.
- Straining: Regardless of whether you are shaking or stirring the ingredients, strain your martini into the chilled cocktail glass.
- Ice:
    - Ice is essential for preparing your martini, but not typically added to your glass.
    - Use ice straight out of the freezer and as dry as possible.
    - Use ice made from fresh (filtered) water.
- Essential equipment:
    - shaker (for mixing or shaking)
    - long-handled bar spoon
    - jigger
    - cocktail strainer
    - extra fine strainer (ideal but optional for any double-straining)
    - lemon peeler
    - martini or cocktail glass
    - cocktail sticks/toothpicks (optional).
- Garnish: A classic martini is traditionally garnished with an olive, but other garnishes are also used, such as:
    - cocktail onion
    - lemon, lime or orange peel (or segment)
    - cherry
    - fresh or dehydrated fruit.

choice of garnish

The options are few when it comes to garnish selection used in a martini. When you consider the other variables in making the perfect martini, this is probably a blessing in disguise. By the same token, there being only a handful of elements required to build the world's most sophisticated cocktail means you shouldn't underestimate the impact of the garnish.

As mentioned, your garnish decision normally comes down to olives, onions or citrus.

why olives?

Who came up with the idea that an olive was the answer to building such an iconic drink? While not glaringly obvious in the first instance, the olive's primary function goes much deeper than simply providing some much needed visual splendour to what would otherwise be a rather naked-looking drink.

The function of the olive (and brine, if used) is to highlight the aromatics of the gin. The olive also needs to marry well with the vermouth and provides a pop of flavour to the martini – not unlike adding a pinch of salt to a savoury dish. The olive has become so integral to a martini that, without it, you no longer have a martini but an entirely different cocktail beverage.

Consider your choice of olive to be the final (but crucial) piece to your martini puzzle. Firstly, ensure your olives are fresh. Nothing sitting at the back of the fridge for weeks on end should be deemed good enough for your creation – they will ruin your martini masterpiece.

Secondly, choose your olives wisely. Typically, green olives are the go-to, but the pimento-stuffed options are not ideal. (The sweetness of the pimento pepper tends to clash with the flavours you're striving for in a martini.) Although certainly not the only the option, the plump, beautiful green Sicilian olives are well worth putting on the short list.

If you dare, play around with olives stuffed with onion, almonds, anchovies or even blue cheese. Depending on the gin you use, these gourmet-style stuffed olives may, in fact, enhance your martini flavour profile – or … they may not. Remember, you're searching for your interpretation of the perfect martini.

Thirdly, your olives must be chilled. Using what's been accidentally left on the kitchen bench at room temperature will unfavourably affect the final outcome (keep in mind that everything in your martini must be chilled).

Remember – the olive makes the martini and, without it, all you have is a cocktail.

Adding brine from the olives makes a Dirty Martini, and brings a pleasingly savoury character to the drink. The key is to add well-strained, quality brine, because this can potentially make or break a 'Dirty'.

choosing your preferred garnish for the perfect martini

Discovering what you enjoy can significantly affect your martini experience, and this is also true for your choice of garnish. As mentioned, your options are usually olives, onions or a citrus. To find your favourite of these (or your favourite mix), try the following easy, three-step process.

Make up six mini martinis with your favourite gin and vermouth. Set one aside as your untouched original. In the other five, add one of the following in each glass:

- olive (I suggest a whole, unpitted Sicilian)
- cocktail onion
- lemon twist
- orange twist
- lime twist.

The untouched original martini is your benchmark. Use this as your guide between the other five garnished samplers. As you taste each garnished variation, make a note of what you enjoy to determine your preferred martini mix.

types of martinis ...

While the experts agree that gin was originally used in the first martini recipe, the vodka craze in America turned the martini on its head, with cocktail bars leaning towards using vodka in the place of gin to accommodate the American palate.

Vodka does tend to provide a smoother, simpler tasting martini, but gin delivers a more complex flavour profile through the botanicals. For this reason – and with the vast range of gins now on offer – martinis have come of age and become truly outstanding in their own right.

Earlier versions of the martini balanced the ratio of gin to vermouth (1:1). Over time, the amount of gin has gradually increased – which is why martini-making has become more and more controversial and, at the same time, more creative and (dare I say) more relaxed.

The following variations are now popular:

- A traditional martini consists of gin and dry vermouth, served cold with a green olive or lemon garnish.
- A perfect martini is made with gin and sweet vermouth.
- A dry martini uses less dry vermouth, while a wet martini uses more dry vermouth.
- Adding olive brine makes a martini dirty.
- If you swap the olive for a cocktail onion, you have yourself a Gibson, and swapping out the gin for vodka will give you a Kangaroo.

But that's just the beginning – more recipe interpretations of the martini exist than for any other cocktail in the world. The Difford's Guide (www.diffordsguide.com), for example, offers over 200 interpretations of this timeless cocktail that are bold (and, in some cases, cheeky) enough to carry the martini name.

To keep it simple, the following are a few of the more classic martini styles that I consider a 'must-try' before you die.

classic dry martini

Ingredients:

60 ml London Dry gin
10 ml dry vermouth
Ice
Olives, or lemon, lime or orange peel to garnish

Method:

1. In a cocktail shaker or jug, stir the gin, dry vermouth and ice together for about one minute.
2. Strain into a chilled martini glass.
3. Garnish with olives or a citrus peel twist.

bradford

A 'Bradford' is a martini that is shaken rather than stirred. Use the same ingredients as in a dry martini.

gibson

The 'Gibson' is a standard dry martini garnished with cocktail onions instead of olives. The first Gibson was created in 1907 at the Bohemian Grove Club in San Francisco. Prepare as you would a dry martini, but change the garnish to cocktail onions.

perfect martini

Ingredients:

50 ml London Dry gin
50 ml sweet vermouth
Ice
Olives to garnish

Method:

1. In a cocktail shaker or jug, stir the gin and sweet vermouth with ice together for about one minute.
2. Strain into a chilled martini glass.
3. Garnish with olives.

wet martini

Ingredients:

60 ml gin
20 ml dry vermouth
Ice
1–2 dash orange bitters (optional)
Olive or citrus peel to garnish

Method:

1. In a cocktail shaker or jug, stir the gin, dry vermouth and ice together for about one minute.
2. Strain into a chilled martini glass.
3. Garnish with an olive or a citrus peel twist.
4. If not 'wet' enough, alter the ratio to 2:1.

dirty martini

A Dirty Martini uses olive brine to offer a pleasant savoury profile to your classic dry alternative. It is an acquired taste, but once you've found the ideal ratio of ingredients, you'll be converted.

Ingredients:

60 ml London Dry gin
10 ml dry vermouth
5 ml of olive brine (add another 5 ml if you want a dirtier martini)
Ice
3 green olives

Method:

1. Thread olives onto cocktail stick.
2. In a cocktail shaker or jug, stir the gin, vermouth, olive brine and ice until the outside of the cocktail shaker feels cold.
3. Taste to check it's sufficiently cold and the dilution is right.
4. Strain the mix in to a chilled glass and garnish with olives.

filthy martini

Ingredients:

60 ml London Dry gin
10 ml dry vermouth
5 ml of olive brine
5 ml fresh lime juice
Ice
3 green olives and citrus peel to garnish

Method:

1. Thread olives onto cocktail stick.
2. In a cocktail shaker or jug, stir the gin, vermouth, olive brine, lime juice and ice until the outside of the cocktail shaker feels cold.
3. Taste to check it's sufficiently cold and the dilution is right.
4. Double-strain by using the strainer in your cocktail shaker and a fine mesh strainer over your glass as you pour the mix into a chilled glass.
5. Garnish with olives and citrus peel.

breakfast martini

Ingredients:

Ice
1 tsp marmalade
50 ml London Dry gin
15 ml Grand Marnier
15 ml aperitif wine
15 ml lemon juice
1 strip of orange zest

Method:

1. In a cocktail shaker, stir ice and marmalade to dilute.
2. Add remaining liquid ingredients and shake well.
3. Double-strain by using the strainer in your cocktail shaker and a fine mesh strainer over your glass as you pour into a martini glass.
4. Garnish with orange zest.

chocolate martini

Ingredients:

60 ml gin (or chocolate gin)
10 ml crème de cacao
Ice
Fresh mint or orange peel twist to garnish

Method:

1. In a cocktail shaker or jug, stir the gin, crème de cacao and ice together for about one minute.
2. Strain into a chilled martini glass.
3. Garnish with fresh mint or twist of orange peel.

one last bonus ...

Stepping away from strict martini traditions for a moment, I couldn't pass up the opportunity to share two of my favourite things – coffee and gin – in one of my favourite interpretations of the world's classiest cocktail, the Espresso Martini.

The Espresso Martini was created in the 1980s by Dick Bradsell, one of London's best known bartenders and modern-day cocktail creators. Bradsell tells the story that he was approached by a supermodel, who asked him to make her a cocktail that would 'wake her up' and, well … keep her up.

As Bradsell was obliged to do, he made her a cocktail with vodka, sugar, coffee liqueur and a shot of espresso. Clearly, it went down a treat and today we are blessed to enjoy a number of variations on this modern-day martini classic.

While the Espresso Martini is traditionally made with vodka, here is my preferred variation using gin that I trust you'll enjoy as much as I do.

espresso martini

Ingredients:

50 ml gin
40 ml fresh espresso
25 ml Kahlua or Tia Maria
Ice
Coffee beans or orange twist to garnish

Method:

1. In a cocktail shaker or jug, shake the gin, espresso, Kahlua/Tia Maria and ice together for about 30 seconds.
2. Strain into a chilled martini glass.
3. Garnish with three coffee beans and/or an orange twist.

CHAPTER 14

cocktail of
the moment:
the negroni

It will hit you like a freight train after four or five.

ANTHONY BOURDAIN

If the great Anthony Bourdain called the Negroni his 'perfect drink', it must be good. An old Italian classic traditionally enjoyed as an aperitivo to open the palate, its intense and unique bite certainly has the ability to kickstart an interesting evening. The Negroni has come a long way since its limited serving as a pre-dinner drink, however, and is now enjoyed as an 'any time' cocktail delight.

The latest resurgence of gin seems to have brought the Negroni along with it. And, of course, any drink worthy of such status only tastes better when it has a worthwhile story to tell.

As with most cocktail folklore, we should never let the truth get in the way of a good story and, in the Negroni's case, the story is somewhat lost in translation. Whether that's because the storytellers have had 'four or five', or because a number of regions fought to claim ownership of their borders, the story of the Negroni's origins appears to take us to Florence, Italy.

In this story, the drink was first constructed at Caffe Casoni in 1919 for Count Camillo Negroni. He was a regular and usually ordered an Americano, made up of Campari, sweet vermouth and soda as his preferred tipple, after spending some time in the United States. Looking for something stronger to drink, legend tells that the Count asked the bartender to fortify his drink of choice. Forsco Scarselli, the bartender at the Caffe, did just that, swapping out the soda water for gin. He also swapped out the lemon twist normally served in an Americano for orange. To consider using any other garnish with a Negroni today would be almost sacrilege.

Count Negroni was himself quite the character, and the stuff of storytelling legend. Whether he was, in fact, a Count is up for debate, as is his choice of career, which has been listed as banker, gambler and even cowboy.

Whatever its origins, the Negroni is now a firm bar (and home bar) favourite. Considered more of a grown-ups drink because of its distinct bitter notes, Simon Difford of the Difford's Guide (www.diffordsguide.com) elegantly describes it this way: 'It takes its depth from the vermouth, is centred by the bittersweet Campari and is made to sing through the vitality of the gin'.

Couldn't have said it better myself.

the perfect negroni

Ingredients:

25 ml London Dry gin
25 ml Campari
25 ml sweet vermouth
Ice
Orange zest to garnish

Method:

1. Stir all ingredients in a cocktail shaker with ice until well blended.
2. Strain into a short glass on the rocks.
3. Garnish with orange zest.

CHAPTER 15

the resurgence of the cocktail

(and its inebriated history)

I distrust camels, and anyone else who can go a week without a drink.

JOE E. ELLIS

As a gin lover, it would be fair to say I wholeheartedly believe gin to be the world's most loved spirit. That theory is well-supported by the fact that more cocktails are dedicated to gin than any other spirit. Open any cocktail book and you'll find gin is an essential key ingredient. Indeed, over a third of the world's top 50 cocktails rely on gin – not a bad statistic for this delicious spirit that the world has fallen in love with all over again. It's now a tipple enjoyed by more people than ever before.

Why? Because it's so damn good.

Gin provides the kind of diversity and depth of flavour that no other spirit can offer. It brings life and character to a drink. Different cocktails are tailored around particular gin styles and even brands, and because gin marries well with so many different mixers and garnishes, the creative scope for mixologists is almost endless.

From a simple two-ingredient cocktail to the more elaborate concoctions, gin provides a sound base upon which to build a sophisticated, unforgettable cocktail drinking experience.

Today, it's hard to keep up with the seemingly endless vault of cocktail creations, with quirky names and humble beginnings. Whether the cocktail option be handwritten on a dusty chalk board in your local corner bar or featured on a classy, high-end cocktail menu, the standard has never been higher – nor has the ability of those talented mixologists who know how to please a crowd with high expectations.

the history of the cocktail

While the history books tend to be a little hazy as to where the first cocktails originated (maybe the historians were a little pickled at the time?), it would seem that the British nailed the concept of mixology with spirits when they came up with punch.

These early versions of punch likely served a useful purpose of softening the edges of the harsher spirits available at the time, making them more pleasing to the palate with the added sweeteners and ingredients – and, therefore, easier to throw down a few. Punch was also not a taxable commodity.

The famous London Coffee House and Punch House was opened in 1731 by a fellow named James Ashley, which (despite the fact that women were most likely tending the bar on his behalf) unofficially launched him as the world's first celebrity bartender. Ashley's innovation supported his love of spirits. He refined the concept of serving punch-style mixed drinks in made to order, individual serves that made the price per drink more appealing for his patrons.

While England may claim fame for creating the cocktail experience, the United States certainly reinvented it. Cocktails as we know them can be reliably attributed to Jerry Thomas, a rather flamboyant bartender from America who wrote the first known bar manual – the *Bartender's Guide* – in 1862. This is deemed to be the first cocktail book of its kind, and documents his own creations and old recipes passed on by word-of-mouth, as well as Jerry's guidelines for mixing drinks. Thomas updated his guide several times during his life and, in 1876, included the first written recipe of the Tom Collins.

Jerry Thomas brought theatre and showmanship to cocktail making, seizing the opportunity to develop elaborate mixing techniques, using flashy bar tools embellished with precious stones and metals, and delivering the cocktail creation with a flair that not only performed the function of getting a drink, but also entertained the patron in doing so. Thomas was so successful that, at one point, he earned more than the vice president of the United States, taking in $100 a week working at the Occidental Hotel in San Francisco.

As Thomas clearly knew, enjoying a cocktail is not just about the drink itself. The experience also relies on the meticulous creation and design, the carefully selected ingredients, the theatre of production, the attention to detail in the presentation and the occasion at which we may be enjoying them.

some all-time favourite cocktails

In the pages that follow, I run through a few of the best cocktails that have stood the test of time for you to try your hand at creating yourself to appreciate and enjoy.

aviation

The Aviation is a gin-based classic cocktail, shaken and strained into a glass.

Created by Hugo R. Ensslin, the head bartender at the Hotel Wallick in New York circa 1916, the Aviation earned its name due to the addition of crème de violette, which gave the cocktail a pale sky-blue colour. As the 1920s rolled in, air travel began to slowly take off, but was a luxury only the wealthy could afford, so a sense of prestige and opulence surrounded this cocktail in its time.

The Aviation is still a high-flying favourite but note that this does pack a punch.

Ingredients:

50 ml gin
15 ml maraschino liqueur
15 ml crème de violette
15 ml freshly squeezed lemon juice
Ice
Maraschino cherry to garnish

Method:

1. Combine all ingredients in an ice-filled cocktail shaker.
2. Shake well.
3. Fine strain into a chilled cocktail glass and garnish with a maraschino cherry.

bee's knees

The Bee's Knees cocktail is a simple and refreshing drink dating back to the good old Prohibition days. The phrase 'bee's knees' was slang during this time for 'the best' (as it still is today).

This cocktail was likely designed to sweeten up an otherwise bitter 'bathtub gin', which was all the rage at the time this cocktail was first made. (Skip back to chapter 2 for more on bathtub gin.)

Frank Meier, the first head bartender at the Ritz in Paris was the creator of the Bee's Knees in the early 1920s. The dominant honey and citrus flavours were used to camouflage the less than ideal gin used, substituting the highly unpleasant smell and taste of the gin for a citrusy sweeter outcome.

While the cover-up may have redeemed a substandard gin back then, the Bee's Knees certainly holds its own today.

Ingredients:

60 ml gin
20 ml freshly squeezed lemon juice
10 ml orange juice, if using*
20 ml honey (or honey syrup)

Ice
Orange or lemon twist garnish

Method:

1. Add all ingredients to a cocktail shaker with ice and shake well, ensuring that the honey dissolves into the liquid mix.
2. Strain into a chilled martini or cocktail glass.
3. Garnish with a citrus zest twist.

* A splash of freshly squeezed orange juice creates an interesting variation on the traditional version.

clover club

The Clover Club is a Philadelphian creation, named after a private men's club with the same name. It was the preferred drink of the members frequenting the Club during pre-Prohibition times.

For half a century people were mad for it, but just as quickly as it was taken up, it was abruptly dropped by the menfolk, who deemed the Clover Club to be a 'ladies' drink'.

In recent years, Clover Club has found its way back into fashion as a cocktail that is not only delicious but also visually stunning. The light, soft pink hues and subtle sweet and sour notes make this a refreshingly beautiful, balanced drink.

Ingredients:

40 ml gin
15 ml lemon juice
15 ml raspberry syrup
15 ml dry vermouth
15 g egg white*
Ice
Raspberry garnish

Method:

1. Shake all ingredients in a cocktail shaker with ice.
2. Strain into a separate shaker and shake again with no ice. (This is known as a 'dry shake', which has the effect of whipping air into the cocktail.)
3. Strain into a coupe glass, garnish with fresh raspberries and get it down!

*The egg white in one egg is about 30 ml.

corpse reviver

You can safely assume the Corpse Reviver is a 'hair of the dog' remedy, designed to be consumed the morning after to help you get over the night before.

One of the earlier creations listed here, this cocktail emerged around the mid-1800s, with the first known recipe for it featured in *The Gentleman's Table Guide*, published in 1871.

The recipe has since been revised and multiplied, with two versions – No 1 and No 2 – featuring in Harry Craddock's iconic 1930 publication of *The Savoy Cocktail Book*. (Harry Craddock was a well-known English bartender during the Prohibition era, best known for his work at the Savoy Hotel in London around the 1920s and '30s.)

Craddock recommended that the Corpse Reviver No. 1 be taken 'before 11 am, or whenever steam and energy are needed', and for Corpse Reviver No. 2, highlighted 'four of these taken in swift succession will unrevive the corpse again'.

Sounds like a fun day out.

Strong but tasty, the Corpse Reviver is well worth the experience.

The following outlines the recipe for the No 2.

Ingredients:

- 20 ml gin
- 20 ml lemon juice
- 20 ml Cointreau
- 20 ml Lillet Blanc
- Dash of absinthe
- Ice
- Lemon peel for garnish

Method:

1. Add all ingredients to a cocktail mixer with ice and shake well.
2. Strain into a chilled coupe glass.
3. Garnish with lemon peel.

french 75

Invented over a century ago, this Parisian classic continues to be a crowd favourite, best enjoyed as a pre-dinner aperitif.

Also called a 75 Cocktail, Soixante-Quinze (Seventy-Five) or simply 75, the origin of its name is somewhat strange. The drink dates back to World War I, when a New York Bar in Paris came up with the idea of mixing gin with champagne. The combination was said to give you such a kick that it was like being shelled by a French 75 (a 75-millimetre military field gun). The firearm had a rate of fire of 15 rounds a minute, and was considered a weapon of choice if France was to have any chance of success in the war.

Since its early creation, the 75 has experienced a number of adaptations in the choice of glass and ingredients used, and has even had a name change (or few). The modern-day version includes the addition of lemon juice, sugar (or simple syrup) and ice.

Ingredients:

30 ml gin
15 ml lemon juice
15 ml simple syrup
Ice
Champagne (or sparkling wine)

Method:

1. Add the gin, juice and syrup to a cocktail shaker and fill with ice.
2. Shake for about 5 seconds.
3. Strain into a champagne flute or tall glass and top up with ice-cold champagne or sparkling wine.

gimlet

The precise story of how the Gimlet was named is unclear, but two theories are reasonably credible and certainly worth sharing.

The first makes reference to the 'gimlet' as a T-shaped tool with a screw tip, used for boring small holes into wood or barrels. The suggestion is that this term was used figuratively to describe the 'penetrating' effects of the Gimlet on the drinker.

The second theory is that the concoction was borne from necessity, and used to help combat scurvy among British sailors on long voyages. In this version of events, the drink was a clever creation by naval surgeon Dr Thomas Gimlette, who had been tasked with the challenge of getting the sailors to take their daily dose of vitamin C as a medicinal preventative for scurvy.

A ship's bulk supply of fresh limes would deteriorate over the long voyages, and they would become almost inedible – which deterred sailors from taking their rations. By mixing the lime with a sailor's ration of gin, not only was the lime made more palatable (as well as the gin back in those days), but the good doctor solved the problem of keeping the menfolk entertained, well rewarded (in gin) and healthy.

It would be hard to find a cocktail easier than the Gimlet to make and with a story (or two) better than the Gimlet's to tell.

Ingredients:

60 ml London Dry gin
20 ml freshly squeezed lime
20 ml simple syrup

Ice
Lime wedge to garnish

Method:

1. Mix the gin, juice and syrup in a cocktail shaker filled with ice.
2. Shake vigorously for 10 seconds.
3. Strain into a chilled coupe glass and garnish with lime.

Note: Numerous variations on these ingredients and their ratios exist, so find the sweetness and balance that works best for you.

gin fizz

Henry C Ramos is the man to thank for the Gin Fizz. The humble beginnings of this delicious creation were in 1888 at the Imperial Cabinet Saloon, Ramos's bar in New Orleans. Originally called a New Orleans Fizz (no guesses as to why) and also referred to by Ramos himself as the One and Only One, this cocktail was such a hit that keeping up with demand was a challenge.

Ramos would employ over 20 bartenders and 'shaker boys' at a time to exclusively make the Gin Fizz. Even so, the drink's popularity – and exceptionally long 12-minute production time – still meant keeping up with demand was a struggle.

While this cocktail has a number of simpler variations, so you can appreciate the original One and Only One, I've included here the Ramos Original Gin Fizz (with a tweak or two).

Ingredients:

50 ml London Dry gin
15 ml freshly squeezed lemon
15 ml freshly squeezed lime
20 ml simple syrup
20 ml egg white*
3–4 drops of orange flower water
2–3 drops vanilla extract
25 ml cream
Ice
50 ml soda water (or a touch more if you need)
Slice of orange for garnish

Method:

1. Add all ingredients (except the soda water) in a shaker without ice and shake well.
2. Fill with ice and shake again for 8 to 10 seconds.
3. Strain into a chilled Collins glass at the same time as pouring in the soda water, enabling both liquids to blend together on the way into the glass.
4. Garnish with slice of orange.

* See note on egg whites in Clover Club recipe.

gin sour

The Gin Sour is one of those cocktails that is likely to have emerged by accident and then become popular enough to end up as a recipe in a cocktail book. The Gin Sour comes from a family of mixed 'sour' drinks that use different base spirits, and pre-dates the Prohibition era in the United States.

Ingredients:

60 ml London Dry gin
25 ml lemon juice
20 ml simple syrup
15 ml fresh egg white
3 dashes of Angostura bitters
Ice
Lemon and/or cherry garnish

Method:

1. Add all ingredients to a cocktail shaker with ice and shake well.
2. Strain into a glass on the rocks.
3. Garnish with lemon (and a maraschino cherry, if that floats your boat).

* See note on egg whites in Clover Club recipe.

jasmine

It's never too late to invent a quintessential modern-day classic – something the Jasmine proves. This cocktail is a mid-1990s creation named after a good buddy needing a new drink to tantalise the taste buds. The story goes like this …

Matt Jasmin walks into a bar and says to his bartender buddy, Paul Harrington, 'Make me a drink that's never been done before.'

Having just pulled together a Pegu Club cocktail for another customer, Paul decided to put a spin on the early 20th century crowd favourite. The result was a drink that is bright, citrusy and zesty, with a touch of tart.

While few creations are an overnight success, the Jasmine eventually caught on – in part because Paul decided to include it in his own cocktail recipe book, *Cocktail: The Drinks Bible for the 21st Century*. (What he didn't do before publishing was check the correct spelling of his good buddy's surname.)

The Jasmine is classically simple and also boozy, perfect for those warm, summer days. And if the Negroni isn't quite your thing, you might find this is a great alternative.

Ingredients:

50 ml London Dry gin
25 ml freshly squeezed lemon juice
8 ml Cointreau
8 ml Campari
8 ml simple syrup (if you like a little sweetener)
Ice
Lemon twist to garnish

Method:

1. Add all ingredients into a cocktail shaker filled with ice and shake well.
2. Strain into a coupe or martini glass.
3. Garnish with a lemon twist.

red snapper

This classic gin cocktail takes its inspiration from the Bloody Mary, one of the world's best-known cocktails that sells itself as a cure-all for hangovers. The Red Snapper is essentially the 'gin' version of the Bloody Mary (which uses vodka). The vodka seems to have been swapped out for gin around the time when vodka was hard to find in the US, which explains why the Red Snapper is a more recent cocktail creation, and why it's seen as a spin-off of the Bloody Mary.

Whether it lives up to its hangover-cure promise or not, a Red Snapper certainly appeals to many and, if nothing else, is a great excuse for a tonic after a groggy start. It's also one of the few alcoholic beverages considered socially acceptable to drink first thing. And if you want to really push the envelope (and depending on the inebriated state of the company you're in at the time of drinking one), you might even be able to successfully argue its value as a nutritional brekky in a glass.

The key to getting this cocktail right is to use quality ingredients. Don't go cheap on the tomato juice and always use freshly squeezed lemon. And whatever you do, don't settle for a limp stick of celery – if ever a cocktail deserves a strong finishing touch, it's this one.

As to how and why this cocktail is called 'Red Snapper', it's a little unclear. To be honest, the naming rights probably belong to someone who was still intoxicated at the time and, quite possibly, a keen fisherman who managed to find the connection between the red colour of the drink and his preferred catch.

The first written reference to a Red Snapper was in *Crosby Gaige's Cocktail Guide and Ladies' Companion*, published in 1941, but this recipe used vodka rather than gin. More recently in the 1960s, it was referred to in a London magazine as 'The Red Snapper – Bloody Mary made with Gin'.

Enough of the history lesson, here's how to make your own.

Ingredients:

2 pinches celery salt
2 pinches freshly ground black pepper
1 lime wedge
Ice
60 ml gin
120 ml tomato juice
15 ml freshly squeezed lemon juice
6 dashes Tabasco
4 dashes Worcestershire sauce
1 celery stick for garnish
1 extra lime wedge for garnish

Method:

1. Mix the celery salt and pepper together on a small plate.
2. Rub the juice from the lime wedge around the rim of a tall chilled glass.
3. Rim the glass with the salt and pepper.
4. Fill the glass with ice.
5. Mix all remaining ingredients in a cocktail shaker filled with ice and mix well, without overdoing it.
6. Strain into your prepared glass, garnishing it with the celery stalk and wedge of lime.

southside

As is the case with most cocktails, the origins of the Southside are shrouded in mystery and subject to much speculation.

While a number of stories are bandied around, what's fairly certain is that it originated on the 'southside' – of where, no-one can be sure, but the shortlist is either Long Island (ho hum) or Chicago during the time of Al Capone (yeah).

Let's go with Al Capone.

In this version of its origins, this cracking cocktail came from the southside of Chicago during Prohibition, drunk by the mobsters living on the southside of town – while on the other side of town, the undesirables would drink a Northside (gin and ginger ale).

To be honest, the Southside looks a little too refined for a gangster – but, hey, let's assume that Al had a softer side.

Whether this is folklore or true remains to be seen, but we shouldn't let the truth get in the way of a cocktail as notorious as this.

Ingredients:

6–8 fresh mint leaves
60 ml London Dry gin
30 ml freshly squeezed lemon or lime juice
15 ml simple syrup
Ice
Fresh mint to garnish

Method:

1. Mix all ingredients in a cocktail shaker with ice and shake well.
2. Strain into a chilled coupe glass.
3. Garnish with fresh mint (but spank it first – refer to chapter 10).

tom collins

One legend about the Tom Collins cocktail claims it started with a prank that quickly gained momentum around New York in 1874. Known as the 'Great Tom Collins Hoax of 1874', a man would tell his friend that someone by the name of Tom Collins was telling tales about him and, if he wanted to confront 'Tom', he could be found just around the corner at the local bar. In an agitated state, the friend would march to the bar looking for the non-existent Tom Collins. That was usually the end of the prank, but one entrepreneurial bartender with a wicked sense of humour decided to make the most of the opportunity and created a drink with the same name. When men came in demanding Tom Collins, he poured them the drink and charged them for it.

Of course, a number of other barmen have also claimed the cocktail as their own and, as you'd perhaps expect, their surnames are all 'Collins'. The best of these contenders is John Collins, a bartender who worked at a Limmer's Hotel in London. In this version, the barman originally used genever instead of gin and called it a 'John Collins'. When the genever was swapped out for Old Tom gin, the Tom Collins was supposed to have been 'officially' born.

Whatever its origins, it's hard to look past the beauty of a Tom Collins. It is so famous it has a glass named after it, and has been the inspiration for countless other cocktails built on its foundation – and justifiably so.

This classic has many variations, but here's my favourite take on the Tommy C.

Ingredients:

75 ml London Dry gin
15 ml lemon juice
15 ml orange juice, if using*
1 teaspoon sugar
Ice
Soda water
Orange garnish (and maraschino cherry if you must)

Method:

1. Add all ingredients (except soda water and garnish) in a cocktail shaker filled with ice and shake well.
2. Strain into a tall glass filled with ice.
3. Top up with soda and garnish.

*Orange juice can be added for an extra touch of sweetness.

one last shot ...

As we come to the end, my hope is that your love for gin has been further fuelled by the words shared with you in this book.

Perhaps this book has allowed you to indulge in your love of history, fuelled your boffin mind, brought out your creative spirit to try a cocktail or few, or even tantalised your palate with a renewed understanding of how to taste gin. Whatever this book has given you, one thing is important to remember – gin doesn't need to be taken too seriously, but it certainly deserves to be respected, appreciated and, above all, enjoyed.

After all, it is the world's most celebrated spirit.

Let yourself be the spirited gin enthusiast, who no longer needs to be drawn – or limited – to the cheapest bottle on the shelf. So many gins are out there waiting for you to discover, with a story to share and a region to connect you to, perhaps with botanicals that have never before been used from places you've never seen. Even let that quirky label be enough to encourage you to give in to your curiosity and give a gin a go.

More than ever before, gin lovers now have the motivation and means to share their gin collections, tasting notes and personal gin experiences with their fellow gin soulmates all around the world. And so do you. All you need is a phone, a photo and a few hashtags. The global gin-loving community is waiting to hear from you and learn more about your thoughts on your favourite gins.

Rest assured – the best part of your gin journey is that your new favourite gin is still out there waiting to be discovered by you. And when you've found it, another will be out there, waiting to be found. There's no right or wrong, just what's right for you.

And that, my gin-loving friends, is the absolute, undeniable, extraordinary, sheer beauty of gin.

Yours in spirit ...

Clare
xxx

gin musings ...

Writing this book is the result of countless hours of reading and researching everything I could find on the topic of gin. Along the way, I stumbled onto some fun facts that simply couldn't be left on my editor's 'publishing' floor. (Actually, some of the musings included here are also mentioned in the main part of the book, but are well-deserving of another mention.)

a touch of history

- Traditionally, stills are named after women.

- Commercial ice was available before electricity.

- Ice balls were invented in 2009 because of gin.

- Rumour has it the royal family cleans their silverware with gin.

- London Dry gin doesn't need to be made in London – it's a style guideline rather than a demographic indicator.

- At one time, 25 per cent of habitable structures in London had a working gin still.

- In the 1720s, London had 1500 working stills and over 6200 places to buy gin.

- Gin is the reason we've grown up with Dr. Seuss. Born Theodor Seuss Geisel, the writer started out as the editor of the college humour magazine *Jack-O-Lantern* during his university years at Dartmouth College – which was also during the time of Prohibition. In 1925, he was caught smuggling gin into his dorm room by the dean and was subsequently fired from the editor's job. Adamant that his writing would continue to be published, he submitted his articles under various aliases – one of which was 'Seuss'. He later added 'Dr.' to this name.

- Gin was once prescribed to treat infections, lung conditions and circulation ailments. Back in the day, it was sold in pharmacies because of its medicinal value.

- The first pink gin was invented in 1826.

juniper musings

- Juniper berries aren't actually a berry, but a cone.

- Juniper is also regarded as a super food, because it is loaded with antioxidants that are effective in fighting infection, aiding digestion and relieving bloating.

- Gin must contain juniper to be legally referred to as gin.

- Throughout the plague in the Middle Ages, doctors wore masks filled with juniper berries to avoid smelling the bad odours that were thought to spread the plague.

- Juniper is a natural flea repellent.

- Very seldom is juniper cultivated on farms – nearly all the juniper berry grown globally is picked in the wild and harvested by hand.

- Juniper was almost endangered due to widespread fungus attacking the juniper berries. As recently as 2017, millions of seeds have been 'banked' to ensure the species does not become extinct.

healthy musings

- Despite what you may have heard, no evidence backs up the suggestion that gin is a depressant. Other than perhaps making you feel a little shoddy and flat after a big gin session, gin is better known for its calming effects.

- All distilled gin is gluten-free. Distillation is the process of separating out the alcohol, and gluten cannot travel with ethanol vapour, so gluten remaining in the distilled spirit is not possible. However, any botanical ingredients containing gluten that have been added to a distilled gin by way of maceration or infusion may have an impact on that gin remaining gluten-free.

- A shot of gin contains roughly 72 calories.

- Gin doesn't have a shelf life. Once opened, it may lose a few of the flavour nuances or diminish slightly in alcoholic strength. But, otherwise, it's good to drink till the end.

- You can't freeze gin.

cocktail musings

- Despite the martini cocktail being around since the late 19th century, the martini glass only got its name in the late 20th century.

- Though James Bond is responsible for the most famous martini quote in the world, bartenders tend to disagree and prefer a martini to be 'stirred, not shaken'.

- The olive as a choice of garnish was popularised by the Americans in the late 1800s.

- No-one knows who came up with the name 'martini'.

- More classic cocktails are made with gin than any other spirit. On top of the cocktails already included in chapter 15, we also have the Gin Rickey, Martinez, Gin Sling, Alexander, White Lady, Hanky Panky, Pegu Club, Silver Bronx, Cosmanaut, Gin Mule (and the list goes on).

a salute to the world's top performers

- More gin is consumed per capita in the Philippines than any other country in the world, with the nation consuming over 50 per cent of the total amount of gin consumed globally (according to a 2013 report by International Wine and Spirit Research).

- Ginebra San Miguel is the top-selling gin brand in the world, selling over 31 million 9-litre cases. Most of this gin is consumed in (yep, you guessed it) the Philippines.

- Over 75 per cent of the active distilleries in Australia, the UK and the US were established after 2009.

- In 2010, the UK had around 90 distilleries. By 2019, it reached almost 700.

- In 2010, the US had around 400 active distilleries – there are now over 2000.

acknowledgements

Gin – for me – is not just about relishing gin in its exquisite splendour. It's also about the social experience, enjoying a tipple or few with gin-loving friends and connecting with new people who hold a like-minded passion for all things gin.

Writing a book about gin during a global pandemic therefore throws some interesting curve balls when bringing such a book to life.

Thanks to some creative manoeuvring, days and nights on Zoom, last-minute pivotal planning and making the decision to just get the bloody book done, it's a humbling experience to see this book finally here.

And of course, no project as crazy as this can happen without the ongoing support and dedication of many others.

Firstly – my flipping awesome family. Thank you for indulging me throughout the book writing process. Thank you for learning to love the art of making kick-arse dinners, hugging and kissing me when needed, keeping me on the straight and narrow, and telling me that it's cool having a mum/wife write a book about booze. Everything I do, endure and work hard for is because of you.

Flagging it now (to soften the blow) – thought you should know there's another book on the way in 2022 (sorry-not-sorry).

To the people who helped me bring this book to life: Michael Hanrahan – it's been my privilege and pleasure to finally work with you throughout this publishing process (with complimentary therapy). Thanks also for patiently listening to some of my crazy stories without judgment and supporting me through the book writing journey.

Anna, Charlotte, Kerry, Karen and the rest of the team at Publish Central – my deepest gratitude to you for caring about the best outcome for this book.

Julie Renouf – I love what you do. Thank you for the energy and colour your talent brings to this book. And ditto for JooLee Levett – it's all in the detail.

Jez Goodale – you delivered excellence – thank you for trusting in me and contributing so generously to this book. Your energy and approachable enthusiasm brings immense value to the industry. We're in exciting times and I look forward to seeing what lies ahead.

To the 'Still Magic' man, Marcel Thompson – thank you for the gift of your own book and your contribution to mine.

Simon and the team at Indigi-Print – over the moon that we could print right here in Melbourne.

To the contributors who generously supported this book visually and trusted me with their wares – Strangelove, the team at Barware.com.au, SummerThyme.com.au – thank you. To Hollie Walton – you are one out of the box. Thank you for your generosity, support and contribution to this book.

And to you – the owner of this book – my genuine gratitude to you for having a copy of *That's the Spirit*. I hope this book brings you value and joy, and puts a smile on your dial.

Cheers
Clare Voitin

about the author

Acquiring her first small farming acreage over 20 years ago significantly changed Clare's life. She experienced many peaks and troughs throughout her farming endeavours but, through these very experiences, she also discovered her passion and purpose – in particular, a love of growing and a respect for the land she feels privileged to use.

Clare has planted over 2000 indigenous trees, shrubs and plants that now thrive on her patch of rural paradise, transforming her farm into a sanctuary for not only the local wildlife, but also Clare.

Sharing in these farming experiences with her three sons has played a fundamental role in Clare's journey, and learning how to work with Mother Nature (accepting that 'She' knows best) has been pivotal in Clare's appreciation of our natural world and all that it has to offer.

Clare is a lover of eclectic pursuits. Never one for fanfare and accolades, Clare likes to just have a go and get shit done. While admittedly being a little disorganised, she loves to come up with a thousand ideas in a day. She's a passionate food grower, published author, marathon runner, lover of the rural outdoors, an advocate for living sustainably and can talk the leg off a chair.

Unbeknown to Clare at the time, her farming endeavours would guide her towards the logical next steps of her entrepreneurial path. After taking a hands-on approach to learning as much as she could about farming and agriculture, Clare's experiences evolved into discovering the sheer beauty and magic of gin.

Clare's appreciation of gin from the production side has been a life-changing experience and a crazy, whirlwind ride since launching Heathcote Gin in July 2019.

What started out as an idea has evolved (rather rapidly) into a well-known and much-loved local Victorian premium craft gin. Through focusing on using the local landscape to inspire, source and grow the botanicals for the Heathcote Gin range, Clare soon realised that the botanicals are where the magic in a bottle of gin begins.

For Clare, creating a regional gin is about more than just the gin in a bottle. It's the journey of exploring new botanicals, and the discovery of how those botanicals might create an amazing, unforgettable gin. With an endless array of indigenous botanicals to be found within Australia's most unique landscape, Clare's ultimate goal for Heathcote Gin is to continue bringing incredible gins to the gin-loving enthusiast.

And just to ensure that Clare continues to follow her mantra of 'getting shit done', it's safe to assume another book (or a few) is on the way.